Praise for Daphne R   D0205033

Praise for *When You Think You're Not Enough*

"The Love Doctor has done it again! In her many books on relationships, Daphne Rose Kingma has written eloquently and wisely on love. Now she turns her attention to the relationship upon which all others are grounded—the love of self. If you're good at giving to others what you most need for yourself, please read this book. You are worth it!"

— MJ Ryan, author of *Attitudes of Gratitude*

"This book speaks to our hearts and souls. Daphne Rose Kingma helps readers root out beliefs and behaviors that limit love of self and others and then, with gentle wisdom, guides us onto a more positive and empowered path. Once I began reading, I couldn't put it down!"

— Sue Patton Thoele, author of *The Courage to Be Yourself*

Praise for *The Ten Things to Do When Your Life Falls Apart*

"Anyone going through a dark night of the soul needs to have this book. It will be your closest companion and your most tender angel. Daphne Rose Kingma more than speaks to your soul; she knows how to heal it."

— Marianne Williamson, author of *A Return to Love*

"What if, during the worst times you can imagine, you felt a warm and steady hand on your back guiding you forward? What if it helped you remember to turn toward what can be possible instead of against yourself or away from what you are afraid of? This book is that hand. Read it and you'll live better."

— Dawna Markova, PhD, co-creator of *Random Acts of Kindness*

Praise for *The Future of Love*

"In this innovative book, Daphne Rose Kingma breaks down the popular myth of how love is 'supposed' to be by introducing us to a broad spectrum of intimate connections. She reveals how to work through the various confrontations that every relationship encounters and reach deeper levels of love and intimacy."

— John Gray, PhD, author of *Men Are from Mars, Women Are from Venus*

"Deeply insightful and daringly fresh, this book takes a breathtaking step away from tradition and into the possibility of saying yes to the true and grandest desire of our being: to love fully."

— Neale Donald Walsch, author of *Conversations with God*

Also by Daphne Rose Kingma

When You Think You're Not Enough: The Four Life-Changing Steps to Loving Yourself

The Ten Things to Do When Your Life Falls Apart: An Emotional and Spiritual Handbook

True Love: How to Make Your Relationship Sweeter, Deeper and More Passionate

Weddings from the Heart: Contemporary and Traditional Ceremonies for an Unforgettable Wedding

365 Days of Love

The Future of Love: The Power of the Soul in Intimate Relationships

A Lifetime of Love: How to Bring More Depth, Meaning and Intimacy into Your Relationship

Finding True Love: The Four Essential Keys to Discovering the Love of Your Life

Heart & Soul: Living the Joy, Truth & Beauty of Your Intimate Relationship

Coming Apart

Why Relationships End
and How to Live Through
the Ending of Yours

Daphne Rose Kingma

Conari Press

This edition first published in 2012 by Conari Press, an imprint of
Red Wheel/Weiser, LLC
With offices at:
665 Third Street, Suite 400
San Francisco, CA 94107
www.redwheelweiser.com

ISBN: 978-1-57324-547-0

Library of Congress Cataloging-in-Publication Data is available on request.

Cover and text design: Jim Warner
Typeset in Adobe Garamond Pro
Cover art: Robert Burridge

Printed in the United States of America
MAL

10 9 8 7 6 5 4 3 2 1

The paper used in this publication meets the minimum requirements of the American
National Standard for Information Sciences—Permanence of Paper for Printed Library
Materials Z39.48-1992 (R1997).

For Nancy
  who believed

For Mary Jane
  who insisted

For Wink
  who encouraged

and

For Leo
  who proved beyond the shadow of a doubt

It is difficult suddenly to put aside a long-standing love
It is difficult, but somehow you must do it.

—Catullus

Contents

A Note to My Readers

THIS IS THE 4TH EDITION of *Coming Apart*. When it was originally written, a "relationship," and especially a marriage, was generally, at least in public, considered to be between a man and a woman. As we now know, a multitude of relationships are between partners of the same gender, and many of these relationships, too, come apart.

Although the relationships profiled in this book follow the male to female configuration typical of the days of its writing, the issues and relationship dynamics apply whether you are a man in a relationship with another man, or a woman in relationship with a woman. The truth is that whether you are in a heterosexual or same-sex relationship, you may find yourself identifying with the person of either your own or the opposite gender in these stories. That's because just like relationships themselves, relationship dynamics are not confined within gender lines.

Above all, this note is an indication that our expression of love in relationships has found many new forms since this book was originally written. Whatever your relationship orientation, may it offer you the insight and comfort you need.

Daphne Rose Kingma
Santa Barbara, California
November, 2011

Introduction to the Revised Edition

WHEN I WAS A GRADUATE STUDENT getting divorced, a colleague of mine said to me: "Well, now you're the kind of person your mother wouldn't want you to have as a friend." I was devastated by his remark. Yet five years later I found myself counseling a number of people who were shocked to find that their marriages, too, were ending. Wondering how he'd ever get through the process, one of my clients asked if there was a book I could recommend to help him navigate these roiling emotional waters. When I realized that there wasn't, I was inspired to write *Coming Apart*.

Although in our hearts we still hold marriage as the form we most want our romantic relationships to take, the truth is that in the years since this book was written we have seen a whole raft of new relationships spring up like mushrooms. We've also seen that along with marrying, people often come apart; that along with falling in love, we frequently end relationships. Whatever your relationship configuration, marriage, living together, or hopeful romance, if it's coming to an end, you'll find your heart hurting, your psyche scrambled, and your world turned upside down.

No matter how many people have already ended a relationship—and millions have—no matter whether you've done it before yourself, the end of a romantic relationship is still one of the absolutely most devastating emotional experiences you will ever go through. It's like a death, except that with a death you at least know for sure that the story is over: there's no going back. With the end of a relationship, however, there are thousands of agonizing opportunities for second-guessing, wondering whether you've done the right thing, asking yourself if you shouldn't try harder, if there isn't some way to rewrite the story so it can have a happy ending.

In the last several decades, divorce, the legal, court-sanctioned break-up of a marriage, has really come out of the closet. Fully fifty percent of first-time marriages end in divorce, and many statistics speculate that the percentage is even higher for second-time marital unions. In spite of the fact that divorce is now a familiar thread in the fabric of our society, there's still a tremendous amount of shame and confusion when a marriage comes apart. And the multitude of "invisible break-ups"—pulling the plug on a living-together relationship or a romance that's barely out of the starting gate—can be equally, if not even more, traumatic. That's because when you're still just exploring the possibilities of a relationship, or if you've been in it for a while and are wondering whether or not to take it to the next level—to start living together, for example, or to turn your living-together relationship into a marriage—the heartbreak can be almost doubled. Not only are you losing the relationship you have, you're also losing the relationship that now you never will have—the one you thought might evolve out of this one.

It's sad but true that overall we're a lot more scared of relationships than we used to be. What seemed in the past like a sure till-death-do-us-part scenario is now beset by circumstances we never used to have to consider: a fragile new economic landscape, a jungle of employment uncertainty, cyber distractions of every ilk, and a just plain terrible shortage of time.

In this social landscape, it's harder than ever to pursue romantic relationships and to nurture them. It's harder to keep a relationship together, and even more difficult—in the midst of all the things we're juggling—to confer an intention of permanence on a budding relationship. We used to feel optimistic about solidifying our relationships, and pretty darn sure about taking the step of marriage. So we were therefore all the more shocked when our marriages crumbled to an end. But now, as if all that weren't enough, added to the new fragility of marriage is the current explosion of alternative relationship forms, making us vulnerable to a whole new array of unexpected endings.

Whether you slipped into a romantic engagement that isn't quite working any longer and are wondering whether it's time to end it, or you were happily grounded in a marriage you were sure would last a lifetime, this book is for you. It's a hand to hold through every agonizing step of the process of letting go. It will tell you how to discover whether or not your relationship has run its course, and what you're likely to encounter as you go through each of the stages of parting. Even more important, it will help you understand why you got into this particular relationship in the first place, as well as what, in the larger frame of your life, was actually accomplished through your being in it. Finally, it will give you practical advice about how to re-gather yourself for the upcoming chapters of your life—even though right now it may be almost impossible for you to imagine that there will be some.

Time does a lot to heal our broken hearts, but really understanding what transpired in each of our relationships is what allows us to finally let go and move on.

No one I've ever worked with who has ended a relationship has come back to me later saying they wished they could resurrect the relationship they struggled so hard to let go of. That's because life keeps taking us to new places. It wants us to continue to grow and so it keeps sending us new people and experiences to enlarge our experience of life and of ourselves. So take heart. Although there may be plenty of tears in the process, you're not headed down a dead-end street. In fact, when you've taken yourself through the process of parting, you may just find yourself standing at the doorway to a whole new life. It is my deepest hope that you will.

1

A Hand to Hold

ENDING A RELATIONSHIP is so painful and makes us feel so awful—bad, hopeless, inadequate, desperate, lost, lonely, and worthless—that most of us are afraid we won't live through it. We feel bad about what our families will think, we're afraid of what the neighbors will think, we feel terrible for our children, we worry about leaving our houses, and we're anxious about our financial futures. But worst of all, we feel badly about ourselves. Not only are we losing context, history, and the familiar choreographies of our lives, but we are also losing a sense of who we really are and we get shaken to the core about our own self-worth.

At precisely the moment when we most need some perspective, some sense that there are reasons besides our own failures to account for what is happening, we are most inclined to take the blame entirely upon ourselves. It is exactly because it is such a natural inclination to define the ending of a relationship as a personal failure—and, consequently, to go through what is often a devastating crisis in self-esteem—that it is terribly important to see that there are always some other factors operating when a relationship ends.

Rather than viewing the end of a relationship as a statement of personal failure, I believe there are always good, legitimate, and understandable reasons why relationships end. These reasons have to do with the chemistry and process of relationships themselves.

In our individual lives, relationships are one of the most important vehicles by which we create our identities and through which we define ourselves. Since this is the case, it may be that we will create a number of relationships to achieve that self-definition, and, consequently, we may end one or several relationships in a single lifetime.

A relationship is a process and not a destination. It is not necessarily the final emotional resting place of the persons who enter into it, but a vital and growing entity that has a life—and a lifetime—of its own.

While we don't give it much thought, our most strongly internalized myth about love is that "love is forever." Our popular music and literature continually assert this, and even aside from this encouragement, we tend to see relationships as permanent, to assume that once they have begun, they will go on, immutably, forever.

And yet, with increasing frequency, relationships do end. One out of every two marriages ends, and uncounted numbers of short- and long-term unions not legalized by marriage also end. These stunning statistics certainly prove that love is not forever, yet when our relationships end, we judge ourselves harshly, according to the values implied by the myth of forever.

The truth is that since we first embroidered this myth on our hearts, our relationships have gone through innumerable transformations, while our thinking about them has not. As a result, an incredible number of people are suffering through the trauma of ending their relationships with guilt, rage, self-flagellation, and a profound loss of self-esteem as the only emotional hallmarks of parting.

We all seem to be experts at falling in love. We even have a number of commonly agreed upon rituals for courting. But we don't know much about what goes on inside of a relationship, and we know even less about how to end one. Survivors of ended relationships haven't left us much of a trail as to how they made it through this painful rite of passage. We know that there are some survivors, that hardly anyone dies or ends up in an insane asylum because of having ended a relationship. Indeed, among the "survivors," we know many examples of transformed men and women, people who are happier after their break-ups and divorces. But we don't know how they made it through the terrible experience.

That's one of the reasons endings are so difficult. We don't know how to do them. We don't know how to get through the endings of relationships. We've all seen people around us going through their endings (or we've even done it once or twice ourselves), and what we see are people in pain, bouncing off the walls emotionally and having to go through radical upheavals in their lives and circumstances. In general, our observations teach us that the endings of relationships are frightening indeed, and this makes us very afraid of going through an ending of our own. Sometimes we are even afraid to acknowledge that the dissolution of the relationship might actually be an improvement because we are so afraid of going through whatever we'll have to go through in order to accomplish it.

One of our greatest fears about ending a relationship is that in the process of parting we will have to experience feelings that will overwhelm us and from which we will never be able to recover. We all suspect that the ending of our relationship is going to take us into some deep emotional waters. We are already feeling vaguely out of control as we contemplate the possibility of the ending, and we sense that the ending itself will take us in over our heads emotionally and leave us feeling totally out of control. This fear is so immense—and so pervasive—that even if a soothsayer could tell us unequivocally that in twenty-five years we would still be as unhappy in our present relationship as we are now, we would probably still be afraid of ending it. Many of us would rather do anything—including continuing to live in a miserable, lifeless, spirit-defeating relationship—than go through all the feelings of ending a relationship.

Another great fear is that, once having ended our present relationship, we will never love or be loved again. While this feeling is very frightening, it has been my experience that, for the most part, this is not the case; in fact, an overwhelming majority of my clients who ended relationships went on to establish new and much more satisfying unions. These happier relationships resulted when people were willing to learn the lessons their previous relationships had to teach.

I have helped hundreds of people through the process of ending their relationships: people who precipitated the ending, people who resented the ending, and couples who mutually agreed upon the ending. My experience is that whether you leave or were left, if you are willing to go through the process of ending in a directed and thoughtful way, without avoiding any part of the emotional process, you can go on to establish a new and more satisfying relationship.

The purpose of this book is to hold out a hand to anyone who is already going through the ending of a relationship and who, as a result, is feeling all the difficult, scary, and unfamiliar feelings that accompany a parting. (If you are not sure your relationship is ending or should end, begin by reading the coda, which starts on page 155.) By showing you that relationships do have legitimate reasons for ending, by guiding you through the normal emotional stages that occur, and by providing you with a first-aid kit for getting through the ending, this book will enable you to live through the end of your relationship with your self and your self-esteem intact.

2

Why Is Breaking Up
So Hard to Do?

NEXT TO THE DEATH of a loved one, the ending of a relationship is the single most emotionally painful experience that any of us ever goes through. In spite of divorce statistics, and although every one of us has been touched by someone's experience of divorce or separation, when we find ourselves contemplating the end of our own relationships, we are totally unprepared. The terrible thing that happens to others is, like terminal illness or death, a thing that is never supposed to happen to us. Because love is our security blanket, we want it to last forever and to be our everything. That's why breaking up is so hard to do.

Existential Fears

When I say that love is our security blanket, what I mean is that we use our intimate relationships more than any other experience in our lives to solve some of the most basic questions of our existence. "Why don't I live forever?" "What is the meaning of life?" "What should I do while I'm here?" We very often want to see our relationships as providing the answers to these questions. To the question "Why don't I live forever?" the answer becomes, "If you love me, it doesn't matter." To the question, "What is the meaning of life?" we answer, "Love." And to the question, "What shall I do while I'm here?" we often answer, "Love my husband, love my wife, enjoy one another till death do us part."

Among the many things that we're continually trying to work out in our lives is the problem that none of us lives forever, that our human existence is finite. Because we are all afraid of death, of the ultimate extinction of our personalities, we do whatever we can to give ourselves stability. We try to provide ourselves with the illusion that some things can always be counted upon, that some things will always continue. We try to defend ourselves against the gaping hole of death by taking love into our lives, by staying close to the persons about whom and to whom we can say, "I know you'll always be with me. I know you won't leave me here alone." Because the thought of death is so intimidating, whatever gives us the illusion of stability and permanence is extremely important to us, and it is to our relationships that we have assigned the primary task of providing us with this sense of permanence.

It is both natural and easy to expect this feeling of permanence from our relationships, because as children most of us experience ourselves as being constantly in relationship to our parents. From the very beginning of our conscious experience, we could feel that they were there, and, so far as we knew, they had always been there. They were there when we opened our eyes, when we first opened our mouths for nourishment, and when, gradually, we generated our first thoughts. Because of this continuous experience of them, our sense is that they are forever, that they always have been, and that they always will be. It is this sense of relationships as continuous and, in a sense, eternal that grants us the necessary stability in our early lives.

For most of us, there was also something immensely luxurious and peaceful about this early experience. Even though as adults we know that our childhood experience of safety was an illusion, we want to create a counterpart experience in adulthood by creating loving relationships, which we hope will serve the same stabilizing function. With our sweethearts, husbands, and wives as our constant protectors, we feel that we are safe. This is also true, in a different way, for people whose parents didn't create a feeling of security in childhood. For them there is a desperate need to establish the sense of security that was always painfully lacking.

One of the reasons we try so hard to duplicate our early experience through our adult love relationships is that in our society there are only two kinds of relationships we believe we can legitimately have. One is as a child in a family; the other is as a grown-up with a spouse. Despite the variety of options that are available to us—living alone, living in a singles' community, living with roommates or friends—at the deepest level of our psyches, we still believe that these are poor substitutes for the real thing: a couple relationship that in its intensity of focus replicates the early childhood experience.

As children, our relationships were fixed; we were inextricably part of a family unit. But, in adulthood, we move into that segment of life where we choose our relationships. We hope to recreate in the format of an adult romantic relationship the feelings of security and connectedness that we experienced as children. When these adult relationships end, we are tossed out into the open sea of nonconnectedness; it suddenly feels as if we are totally alone. We can't go home and be little children again, so when we end our adult relationships, we feel as if we have separated ourselves from the only context and format we believe we're allowed to have as a safe harbor in our adult lives. We feel emotionally devastated.

Obsolete Mythologies of Love

Another thing that makes breaking up so painful is that we have a number of myths about love and relationships, about how love and marriage "should be," that are no longer a reflection of reality. Our beliefs about love no longer match up with what's going on in the world, and they are contradicted when our relationships end. I call these out-of-date notions the obsolete mythologies of love.

Love Is Forever

Our primary and probably most potent myth about love is that love is forever, that when we make a relationship, it will last for our whole lives. Our marriage vows—"Till death do us part"—are the public ceremonial expression of that myth. We don't say, "I'll love you as long as it feels good," or, "I'll love you until I find somebody else." We say, "I'll love you forever; I'll live with you until one of us dies." We expect the person we choose to be our partner for our whole lives.

It is this assumption in particular that makes breaking up so hard to do. In ending a relationship, we negate the myth of forever; we violate the assumption that our relationship will last us for our whole lives. What we see is that instead of being forever, our relationship was just an episode.

Because almost all of us have subscribed to the myth of forever, when our relationships end, the only thing we can say is, "I must not be any good; there must be something the matter with me. I created this relationship with the intention it would last forever, but now it's ending. It certainly can't be ending because the idea that love is forever is wrong, so it's got to be me who is wrong." We spend an unbelievable amount of time in self-flagellation because we can't imagine that the notion of forever could possibly be inappropriate. But it is. There isn't a person in the United States who hasn't witnessed a divorce or the heartbreaking end of a romance. The truth is that relationships end. It is high time we explode the myth that love is forever, so that when we end relationships, we can do so without such devastating crises in self-esteem.

Love Is All-Inclusive

Another one of these obsolete myths is that relationships are all-inclusive. When we make a relationship with someone, we assume he or she will be sufficient to meet all our needs. In other words, we believe that the person we love will be the one person with whom we always go to movies, with whom we always go out to dinner, with whom we go to church, with whom we have all our conversations about our bad day at the office or our ailing back, who knows all our troubles and to whom we unburden ourselves.

We don't enter into relationships saying to ourselves, "Well, in my relationship I'm going to handle my needs for sex and a Friday night date, but I'm going to have an intellectual life with my friend Sally and a cultural life with my friend Stan." When we enter into a long-term relationship, we generally assume that the person we love will be sufficient—or almost sufficient—to meet all our needs. We expect that 95 percent of our needs will be met in our primary relationships and the other 5 percent—well, we'll just forget about them.

We presume the person we love will provide us with companionship and entertainment, with intellectual and emotional stimulation, with physical solace and sexual satisfaction, that he or she will be our . . . everything. We think of a relationship as an exclusive and all-encompassing resource, and we conduct our lives according to this expectation. We begin by turning to our partners and constricting our outreach to others. More and more, we ask our partners to meet all our needs, until they become the focus of our existence.

It is because we have such all-encompassing and exclusive expectations for our relationships that we are devastated when they end. At the simplest level, who will be our Friday night date? How will we meet all our needs—for sex, for conversation, for succor, for daily companionship, and for consistency? What or who will provide the ground of familiarity in our lives? How can we replace the handy-dandy, live-in jack- or jill-of-all-trades that the person to whom we were related had inevitably become?

The great cafeteria of needs that were being met with affection and efficiency by the single person we chose to hold close in our lives is now no longer being met. We are paralyzed not only by thoughts of loneliness—"What will I do for companionship now?"—but also by the aggravation of needing to learn, on what feels like a moment's notice, how to meet all our needs in a variety of other ways.

What's ironic about the forever and the all-inclusive myths is that they sprang up in times when the life span was half of what it is today. In those days, when a person said, "I'll love you forever," forever could be two years or ten years, but it very seldom approached the forty, fifty, or sixty years of marriage that could conceivably be possible today. But even in the past, people often had multiple relationships. They could get married and easily say, "until death do us part," because death often did part them, and the surviving partner would go on to marry again. Relationships ended not because of what occurred within them, but because of external circumstances. It wasn't necessary to ask, "Was I a bad person?" "Did I fail?" "Did this relationship end because I wasn't okay?" None of these questions had to be asked because the usual cause of the ending—death—was out of everyone's hands.

When we apply these myths to ourselves now, however, they can only have one psychological result: we find ourselves in a crisis of self-esteem because we are unable to build relationships that are in accordance with these myths.

The circumstances in which we find ourselves today are very different from those that spawned our cultural attitudes toward relationships, and these mythologies didn't always have such personally negative effects. In the past, the continent needed taming, and its subjugation was best accomplished in community, by teams. The teams began with a pair of people who fell in love or married for convenience and then had children, developing a society and workforce that could get the tasks done.

People were too poor and too busy to worry about anything except economic survival. The point of a relationship was, above all, to establish a stable economic unit, which, with the efforts of all its members, could create a somewhat comfortable life. Once you chose a partner, you just made it work. There was no worrying about the emotional well-being of your relationship or whether you felt good about yourself.

But now our relationship tasks are different. Since as a society we are no longer concerned with conquering the environment, but rather with keeping peace and preserving the environment we have already subdued, we are now turning our attention inward, to deal with the questions of who we are as human beings and what is the meaning in our lives.

In the past, individuals subjugated themselves to the needs of the relationship in order to accomplish work, some task that was a mutually agreed-upon goal. Now we live in a time when relationships exist to serve the deepest needs of the individuals in them.

In a sense, we are asking the relationship to subjugate itself to the evolution of the individual. Because we have solved the issues of basic survival, we have the luxury of moving on to deeper levels of development: emotional, spiritual, aesthetic. And it is in relationships, the intimate and challenging encounter with another, that we do this. This is not a state of affairs toward which we are moving; it is the place at which we have already arrived.

This is a difficult concept for us to admit to ourselves, despite the impact of the "me generation." All evidence to the contrary, we have not yet consciously acknowledged the degree to which we value the development of the self. But it is true that we enter into relationships primarily to discover, foster, enhance, and sustain our individual selves. We haven't really openly acknowledged this because we don't like to think of ourselves as selfish or self-oriented. There is a certain part of us that wants to believe we hold human communion and, therefore, relationships as a higher value than self. We don't like to conceive of ourselves as being in relationships to get something—that's too crass. It also violates our soft romantic sensibilities. We don't want to believe that we fall in love in order to get something out of it.

We want to hold love out as the one part of life where there is still magic and mystery, where there is still romance. Although love does serve to meet our needs for magic, mystery, and romance, the deeper truth is that we all enter into relationships for very specific reasons, whether we choose to see them or not.

In spite of the progress of civilization, relationships are still task-oriented. When we fall in love, we fall in love with the person who will help us accomplish something—whether that's something we know we're trying to accomplish, like getting a college degree or having a family, or whether that's something about which we are entirely unaware, like trying to achieve emotional security.

I am certainly not saying that we should take the mystery, the magic, or the romance out of falling in love, but we certainly do need to take the mystery out of falling out of love. When a relationship ends, it is vital to look at it through reality-colored glasses and ask, "What was it really about?" "What were we doing together, anyway?" We need to see what happened so that we don't feel guilty, so that we learn for the future, so that we can love again.

My experience in helping hundreds of people go through the painful process of parting is that it is only when we truly understand the meaning of our relationships—the tasks we undertook in them, the gifts we received from them—that we can survive their endings with our selves and our self-esteem intact.

3

Exploding the Love Myths: Why Are We Really in Relationships?

J OHN AND DEBORAH FELL IN LOVE when they were both in their late twenties. They'd both had a number of puppy love relationships and were now eager to settle down. He'd been out of college for a couple of years and now was working as a bank management trainee. She was just finishing college.

They had a number of friends in common. She was attracted to his steadiness—"He was so peaceful and comforting"—and he was drawn to her liveliness and affection—"She really adored me." The shy beginning of their romance ("I was the one who called him for our first date," Deborah confessed) flowered into a series of dates and excursions, mutual appreciation of one another, and the feeling that there was no reason whatsoever why there shouldn't be more—a lifetime of what already felt so good to them. After living together in peace and delight for more than a year, they decided to get married.

When Marie and Neil fell in love, everyone thought they were the perfect couple. Neil was a dashing 6'5"; Marie was a dazzling, willowy blond.

"It was love at first sight," according to Marie. "He was just my type of man, grown-up, handsome, accomplished. He met all my criteria for a mate, and when he chose me in return, it was more than I ever could have asked.

"It wasn't just surface, either. We had a lot of things in common. We were both in business. He was a few steps ahead of me when I was starting out and available to give me the guidance I needed. He was my hero and my colleague. My ideal. I felt like the luckiest woman in the world. Six months later, we got married."

In general, when we tell the stories of falling in love, they follow a very specific format: They fell in love, got married, and lived happily ever after. In our unconscious mythologies of love, we see marriage—the cementing of a relationship through the ceremony of marriage—as a destination. We assume that marriage itself is the goal. We assume that love will drop us off at the doorway of a committed relationship and that once we have walked through it, all will be well. More of the same until the end of time. We expect that the high-riding, ebullient, positive feelings that cause us to fall in love will sustain us through all the years of our relationships, that love will dissolve our differences and conquer all. We presume, in a sense, that relationships are about the supremacy of love, that they will meet all our needs and last forever.

However, as the very existence of this book testifies, there is more to a marriage than simply setting it up. A lot goes on in the house of love and, rather than being a destination, relationships are often just a roadside inn, a stopping place on our journeys through life.

So if relationships aren't, in the end, about living happily ever after, about love that conquers all, then what are they really about, you may ask. Why do we really fall in love?

The reason we fall in love is to help us accomplish our external and internal developmental tasks.

Developmental Tasks

In our lifetimes, we are each trying to do a single thing: to create our selves. We are all trying to solve our basic psychological problem—which is to answer in depth and to our own satisfaction the question, "Who am I?"

What this means is that as we proceed through our lives, we are all trying to get a sense of our own identity. In order to do that, we create a series of life experiences that either help us discover who we really are or confirm who we have discovered ourselves to be. This process of self-definition or self-discovery occurs through what I call "developmental tasks," and it is our relationships, more than anything else in our lives, that help us accomplish the developmental tasks through which we define ourselves. That's why we choose the people we do and that's why they choose us. That's also why relationships begin and end.

Developmental tasks are stepping stones in the developmental process. Learning to walk after learning to crawl is a developmental task for an infant, just as attending college after completing high school is an intellectual developmental task for a young adult. The completion of each of these tasks marks the putting into place of another piece of the personality, a further identification of the self, a further coming to terms with who one really is.

Whether we are consciously aware of this or not, we are all, at any given moment in our lives, engaged in this developmental process. We're all going about the business of becoming, or trying to become, ourselves. We're all trying to grow up and leave home: to get educated, to decide whether or not to have children, to survive financially, to solve our addictive problems, to pursue our artistic impulses, to integrate our sexuality, to enhance our self-esteem, to get recognition. All of these are developmental tasks, and we look for whatever assistance we can find to move through one particular developmental stage and into the next.

There are several kinds of developmental tasks. One set is very external and task-oriented. It has to do with what we are trying to accomplish, achieve, or cause to happen at any given moment in our lives: for example, learning to walk, learning to read, leaving home, going to college, starting a business, having a child, building a house.

Another kind of developmental task is a psychological developmental process, where the tasks have to do with our personal psychologies. In this process, the set of tasks has to do with solving some emotional problems, such as taking possession of our sexuality, our anger, our masculinity or femininity, our personal power, our creativity, or self-sufficiency, to name a few.

Since we are human beings, the most natural form of assistance for us is other human beings, and relationships are the most natural from of obtaining the assistance of other human beings. Love is the medium whereby we offer one another this assistance, and, by this definition, a good love is one in which a fairly equal amount of assistance is being given and received by both partners.

This doesn't seem like a very romantic view of love and may even be seen as selfish. But the truth is that the creation of our selves is what is really occurring under the charmed umbrella of our romantic relationships. Rather than being selfish, this is a definition of love that provides an opportunity for real appreciation of the special qualities of both participants. In this sense, it is the fullest view of love.

While relationships very often help us achieve our external developmental tasks—and we often have a very obvious awareness that this is happening ("He helped me finish college," or, "She helped me start my business")—what is of more interest, and perhaps of more importance, is that relationships help us accomplish our emotional developmental tasks. They do this because they are by their very nature emotional. We tend to overlook what we accomplish emotionally in relationships because in general we are not aware of the emotional processes in our lives. But the fact is that consciously or unconsciously we all are always in a state of emotional evolution, and nothing spurs our emotional development more than our intimate relationships.

Since external developmental tasks are pretty much self-evident, I am not going to spend much time talking about them here. What I do want to make clear is the nature of our psychological developmental tasks because they affect our personalities so profoundly.

Psychological developmental tasks in relationships fall basically into two categories: (1) making up for specific deficits from childhood and (2) discovering the emotional meanings of our childhood stories.

Most of us don't treat our personal pasts as being in any way important except perhaps as the foggy preface to the lives we're living now. We tend to think of childhood and adulthood as two distinctly different episodes of self, not as a single continuous lifetime with the threads of childhood woven deeply into the fabric of the present. As a result, we tend to give ourselves very simplistic reports about our childhood: "Of course I was happy; my parents did everything they could," or, "It was awful, but so what—it's over now."

No matter what we'd like to believe, we do carry our childhoods within us. In fact, they are the blueprints for all that follows, and, for the most part, we live our lives as adults based on emotional patterns we learned as children. Both consciously and unconsciously, with unerring accuracy, we make decisions in our adult lives that are our attempts both to understand and to heal what occurred in our early years. Our relationships, more than anything else, are the vehicles by which we try to understand the meanings of our childhoods.

This is difficult for many people to accept, and, in general, we don't like to investigate our childhoods. We think it is a waste of time or we're afraid that if we do examine our childhoods, we will discover our parents' flaws and end up stranded in a state of judging and criticizing them. Since intuitively we know that no parents can do the job perfectly, we don't know what to make of the failures we may uncover.

While it's true that no set of parents is perfect, our exploration is designed neither to give our parents an A for their work nor to level them with our judgments. Rather, it is an opportunity for us to evaluate their deep and abiding impact on us in order to have a more complete understanding of why we live our lives as we do and choose the partners we do. All information is good information because the more we know about ourselves, the more we become capable of being ourselves in the fullest and most holy sense.

Deficits from Childhood

Now let's take a deeper look at the two love stories at the beginning of this chapter. If we look at John and Deborah, for example, and why they really fell in love, we can see that they came together to heal emotional wounds from childhood.

John grew up in a family where his father, a corporate executive who worked eighty hours a week, was rarely home. Even as a child, John was left to take care of his mother. He took on the role of being her companion. He supported her intellectually by enjoying her achievements and emotionally by comforting her when she was sad. Without knowing it, he took on an adult identity much sooner than was appropriate. Not only did he not have a father who was a model for his development as a man (aside from the model of excessive work), but he also did not have a mother to take care of him. In fact, he had a mother he had to take care of, a mother to whom he became the surrogate husband.

When John arrived at adulthood, he had already had a long apprenticeship as an adult. He had a lot of experience making sure that the woman in his life (his mother) was calm and content. He was a wizard at making sure the lawn was cut, the trash was out, the doors were locked, and, eventually, as he reached adolescence, that the bills were paid and his mother had a dinner date.

There were a few things missing, however. John arrived at adulthood without ever having had the experience of simply being loved: being doted on and indulged, being held, caressed, and treated with special deference. He had missed the basic, unequivocal, unconditional love, affection, and approval that, ideally, parents give to their children.

Deborah, an immigrant, grew up in deprivation. Her father was an alcoholic, and, as a result, her mother had become the breadwinner of the family. Her mother, feeling guilty about her husband's alcoholism and her own continual absence, indulged her children materially, giving them everything they wanted. With gifts she tried to make up for what she was unable to give by being home and present to her children's emotional needs. As a result, Deborah grew up thinking that, materially at least, she'd get whatever she wanted, and so in spite of the severe emotional deprivation of living with an absent mother and an alcoholic father, she was a spoiled child.

When she met John, she was immediately attracted to what she called "his grown-upness." A traveling furniture salesman, he seemed to know a lot about life and how to function in the outside world, things she had never learned because her mother had been too busy and her father had been too drunk. She had goals, educational goals in particular, that she had been too unfocused to pursue, and when she told John about them, he encouraged her.

He was, of course, a very grown-up person because he'd been taking care of his mother for years. As a result, he was both able to provide stability and consistency at home for Deborah and to teach her a lot about life in the outside world.

With John, Deborah explored and expanded her skills, and he continued to encourage her. He taught her how to apply for student loans, how to write a job résumé, how to get financing for a car. He even taught her housekeeping skills, like how to make the bed and do the grocery shopping—all the things her mother had been too busy to teach her. In effect, he became both the mother and the father she had never had.

Because she was truly able to receive all John gave her, she felt an immense sense of gratitude toward him. Her mother's indulgence had taught her one important thing—and that was how to be generous. As a result, Deborah gave John what he had never received from his mother. She bought him big and little presents, just as her mother had done for her. She told him he was wonderful and she couldn't live without him, and she specifically praised him for all he did for her.

In this relationship, Deborah was growing up; that was her developmental task. She was learning the skills she would need as a grown-up, so she could function in the world. John was also fulfilling some deficits from his early life. Finally he experienced what it was to be appreciated and loved, to have some attention directed toward him.

Although Deborah and John may be unaware of the reasons why their relationship works, many relationships have as their *raison d'être* and their chief developmental task the completion of growing up. This is because many of us are not well parented. Perhaps we came from families where there were too many children, so our parents didn't have the time or the energy to teach us the skills we needed or to give us the emotional attention we needed. Maybe our parents were committed to the American dream of affluence and success to such a degree that the project of child raising became a very secondary undertaking. Many of us were unwanted children, children who absorbed the blame for crises in our parents' marriage or children about whose very existence our parents felt profound ambivalence. Whatever the reason, many children arrive at adulthood with severe emotional deficits of their own.

"It was a damn disaster," one father said to his daughter, "when you were born. I'd just come back from the war, I was trying to go to college, and then you came along. I had to work two jobs and your mother was always exhausted."

Because of the necessity of providing and burgeoning career opportunities now available to women, many parents are so preoccupied they don't have the time or desire to impart a number of physical, practical, or intellectual skills to their children. As a result, many of us come into adulthood without a lot of the skills we really need to possess. We don't know how to make our way in the world emotionally or practically because our parents, either through circumstances or some deficiency of their own, simply could not or would not teach us what we need to know.

We may be unparented in terms of self-esteem, personal motivation, or the capacity to express our emotions, particularly anger. We may be unparented in the ways of the world—"This is what a loan is," "These are what interest rates are," or, "This is what business is all about." We may be unparented in terms of our health, personal hygiene, nutrition—how to enjoy and value our bodies. Or we may be unparented in terms of organization, how to make decisions, how to use our time wisely, and so forth.

Since no one set of parents can teach us everything, when we arrive at adulthood, we may well have never attained great portions of what we need in order to be ourselves. It's as if we've arrived at the doorstep of adulthood with our little overnight satchels only to find our bags have rips and holes in the bottoms, and we're not very well prepared to live at the grand hotel of adulthood. Our loving relationships are where we patch, mend, and repair the overnight bags of our childhood, so we can live in dignity and comfort in adulthood.

Discovering Our Personal Stories

Let's turn now to the other love story, Neil and Marie. Theirs is an example of a relationship that gives the gift of identity, and it shows how each partner can learn when valuable snippets of information from childhood turn up.

Marie was the youngest in a family of five children. She adored her older brother who, because he was so much older, was like a second father to her. Her father was gone a lot, so it was easy to replace him with her brother, who was also handsome and powerful.

Marie was always trying to get in her brother's good graces, to have him admire and adore her in the ways a father would. But by the time she arrived on the family scene, her brother had already coped with three other sisters. He was bored with being a brother, and, according to him, his pack of younger sisters was a nuisance. They were "into girl things." They were trouble.

Since Marie was the youngest, she received the brunt of his irritation. "Your dolls are in the way again," he would yell. "When will you ever grow up?!" The whole time she was admiring him for being big, grown-up, and handsome, he was putting her down for being little and a girl.

Interestingly enough, Neil had also been an older brother to a series of younger sisters. Neil's sisters had all been spoiled by a mother who always told Neil to set aside his own needs on their behalf. "Just remember they're girls," his mother would say. "They can't help it."

What Marie discovered in therapy was that her relationship with Neil was a replay of her relationship with her older brother. In fact, in their relationship, both Neil and Marie had recreated the roles they had played in their families. Neil became impatient and overly critical; Marie felt victimized and complained that he was always picking on her. Without knowing it, Marie recreated the role of the little sister who absorbed all the negative comments and criticisms of her irritated older brother (in this case, played by Neil, her irritated husband), while Neil was venting his years of buried resentment about the special privileges of women, as first exhibited by his three younger sisters.

This example shows how, consciously or unconsciously, sooner or later, most of us make sure that we watch the movie of our childhood. As one of my woman clients said, "I can't believe it, but my father was an alcoholic, my first husband was an alcoholic, and lo and behold, I've just discovered that my second husband is an alcoholic too."

Another client, a man, said, "My father was an intractable bully, and so is my wife. I was always in a power competition with my father—which I could never win—and now I'm in a power competition with my wife. I can't win this time either. It floored me to realize that I'd married someone just like my father."

As this story illustrates, relationship dynamics don't always follow conventional gender lines. For example, Liz realized that in her husband, she had married a man who behaved exactly like her mother. "My mother was in charge of everything," she said. "She wore the pants. I married a man whose strength I admired, and then I realized that, just like my mother, Bob had to be in control of everything. He had to know my every move, had to make all of my decisions, had to make sure I never had any power of my own. I always thought women married men like their fathers—but my father was so gentle that I could never understand why I always felt so oppressed by my husband. Then, one day I realized that in marrying Bob I had married my mother!" These are all examples of people living reruns of their childhood movies and finally seeing the information they contain.

As the examples of John and Deborah and Marie and Neil demonstrate, whether or not we are aware of it, we form relationships to accomplish our developmental tasks. It follows naturally that relationships will often end because these developmental tasks have been completed.

In the case of John and Deborah, their relationship ended because their emotional wounds from childhood were finally healed. John served as a parent to Deborah, helping her incorporate the skills of adulthood into her life. Gradually, she became a capable, functioning, and self-sufficient adult. The more she applied the skills she learned from John to the pursuit of her own goals, the farther away she moved from him. In time, she began to resent his control. In fact, it became clear that aside from his parenting function, which was now becoming irrelevant, John and her had little in common. Indeed, their worlds scarcely overlapped, and like any other well-reared adolescent, after she'd learned the skills of adulthood, Deborah wanted to leave home.

As for John, he finally received the love he needed in order to know that he was valuable in himself. Being doted on, adored, and spoiled by Deborah filled a longstanding emotional deficit of his. He finally got a crack at the emotional indulgence he had missed as a child. Now that this void had been filled, he longed to use his adult skills on his own behalf. He realized that for years he had put aside his own career in order to focus on Deborah's growth. After she walked out on him, he bounced back with remarkable swiftness. With venture capital borrowed from a business colleague, he started his own foreign car dealership.

Why did Marie and Neil's relationship end? When their fights became too frequent, they entered therapy, and it was there that they realized they were each simply repeating the roles they had played in childhood. Marie realized that in order to be loved by a man she didn't have to repeat the pattern of absorbing criticism and put-downs that had been the hallmark of her relationship with her brother. Neil contacted his feelings of resentment about women, which he had handily delivered to Marie. They were both able to acknowledge these things, to reveal them to one another, and to realize that their relationship had been of tremendous value. Through the repetition of the emotional configurations of their childhoods, they were each able to feel, express, and identify feelings that had long been buried. But after this task had been completed, they found that their relationship really had no life—no common ground, no shared interests, not even a similar set of values. Their parting was sorrowful but gracious.

As these examples show, relationships can end gracefully when the developmental process is complete for both partners. But when the completion is not simultaneous, endings are particularly painful. It may be clear to you that you have completed your developmental task, and you may be aware, at the same time, that your partner has not. That's where guilt comes in.

If you find yourself in this situation, it is important to remember that you can't necessarily make the completion happen for the other person nor must you feel guilty if the other person hasn't finished his or her task. Our developmental tasks are our own responsibility. If we don't complete them, that's our own problem.

An example of this is Sally and Paul. After seven years of marriage, Sally was totally frustrated with Paul's inability to talk, his unwillingness to fight, his refusal to seek counseling, and his general and long-term depression. After a year of therapy herself, she ended the marriage in a unilateral decision that devastated him.

Between the time she decided on the divorce and when it actually occurred, Sally was overcome with guilt. She was worried about her daughter, who had a close relationship with Paul, and she was afraid that there might have been some opportunity for reconciliation that she had overlooked. Perhaps if she pleaded more strongly, somehow he would be willing to change so they could have a workable marriage. But no matter what she suggested, he refused. "I'm happy with the way things are," he said. "If you're not happy, that's your problem."

When he said this, she realized that there really wasn't any hope and proceeded with the divorce. Paul continued to "not understand" what had happened: "You've made up your mind; there's nothing I can do," he said. "I never wanted this divorce; I'm just your victim."

Years later, when his second marriage was ending (as he explained, "for all the same reasons"), Paul finally entered therapy himself. He was finally able to tell Sally what he was learning about his deeply buried anger at his mother and how he had applied it to every woman in his life. "I'm sorry," he said. "I loved you; I just didn't love myself, at least not enough to learn what I needed to in order to keep our marriage alive."

What this story shows is that sometimes the lessons are very long in being learned. It wasn't until fifteen years later that Paul's second divorce finally caused him to discover the unconscious blueprints by which he had conducted his life. Finally, at almost age fifty, he was completing his emotional developmental task.

What happened to Paul is an example of what tends to occur when people fail to understand what they were doing in their relationships: they keep on repeating the pattern until they learn its lesson. That's why so many people who get divorced and remarried find themselves having the same fights, the same dynamics, and the same disillusionments a second or even a third time. They never figured out what they were trying to accomplish in their first marriage and so they had to do it all over again.

Not every relationship changes every person to an equal degree. For many people, relationships are simply a resting place, a "holding tank," where not much significant forward development is accomplished, but in which a certain state of being is allowed to continue uninterrupted. Sometimes this uninterrupted state of being is a kind of growth in itself. As one man said at the end of his relationship, "Ruth was disappointed because I wasn't ambitious; but I couldn't be ambitious then. I'd been through so much in Vietnam that what I really needed was a quiet place. I needed the same person to come home to every night. I needed reality to be unruffled and boring. I needed to cool my heels and get my bearings. In a sense, that was her gift to me: she gave me a place to vegetate for a while."

Relationships also end when the developmental process gets out of joint. A relationship can continue for only as long as the two people in it are either in a parallel or similarly focused developmental process. But when one partner wants to change the agenda and the other prefers the status quo, there's trouble.

For example, Mike and Karen, both high school dropouts, met when they worked at an electronics factory. They were both movie fanatics and played on the company softball team. Since they had grown up in poverty, each dreamed of owning a home. After a two-year courtship, they got married. In order to save money to buy a house, Karen supported Mike while he went through training to become an electrician. They pooled their resources, and within four years they bought their first house.

After three more years they had two children, and Karen began to be discontented. Now that she was at home with the children, she missed the stimulation that in the past her work had afforded. She also realized that for most of her life she had been pressed into the caretaker role. As a child, she had had to take care of her sick grandmother, an experience that now caused her to resent staying home with the children. She realized she wanted to go back to work, but when she discussed this with Mike, he became irrationally enraged.

Mike was from a broken home, and it was very important to him to be the provider for his family. He'd been willing to have Karen work while they were saving to buy the house. But now that it was theirs, he believed her place was in the home. He wanted his children to have a stay-at-home-mother, the way he never had.

At this point, Mike and Karen's process began to be distinctly out of joint. They no longer had a common purpose. When they were both working toward buying a house, they were the perfect partners for each other. But as Karen pressed forward with her psychological need to develop her own capabilities, Mike's dream of a traditional family was threatened. After a year of discussion, bargaining, and pleading, Karen delivered an ultimatum: whether he liked it or not she was going back to work. Declaring that she was an unfit mother for the children, Mike took the two boys and moved out.

What I am trying to show in all these examples is the profound impact of childhood on adult relationships. Without realizing it, we often choose partners who will help us trace back through the dark woods of our childhood, like Hansel and Gretel, picking up the scattered crumbs of our identities along the way. It never ceases to amaze me how little most people know about their own childhoods by the time they reach adulthood, the altar, or the divorce court. For all of us, childhood is the archaeological site from which all the important information about ourselves can eventually be excavated: our hopes, our deficits, our expectations, our personal myths about love and sex, our beliefs about the opposite sex, our sense of self-worth, our feelings about our bodies, and all the thousands of other perceptions and beliefs that form our self-concept.

Most of us move into adulthood essentially uninformed about ourselves, unconscious about all of the influences, persons, and scenarios that have shaped us. As a result, we try to design the experience of adulthood on a conscious level, but also, and more importantly, we try to design the experience of childhood on an unconscious level, in such a way as to recreate what has already occurred so that we can finally understand it.

That's why we frequently see women who as children were abused by their fathers marry men who beat them. It also explains why men who had aloof, unaffectionate mothers often marry women who are physically and emotionally distant.

For every single one of us childhood is the first run of the most important movie of our lives. It would have changed our whole lives if we could have seen it when we were young, but unfortunately we missed it the first time around. Years later, we catch the rerun at another theater—in our love affairs and marriages.

For almost all of us, the vital information about our childhood that we absolutely must have comes only with our adult relationships. Magically, unconsciously, we take the scenarios and emotional dynamics that existed in our relationships with our parents and recreate them in our relationships with our sweethearts, lovers, husbands, and wives. It's as if we're saying to ourselves, "I'll have to do this again until I get it right."

There are a couple of theories about the repetitive psychological patterns in which we all seem to engage. One is that we are all hopeless incompetents and masochists. We just keep doing the same rotten, miserable things over and over because, at heart, we thrive on misery. The other theory is that we keep creating a rerun of our childhood movie because we're trying to understand it, to get the information we missed the last time around (or the first time around). This theory holds that we reenact, recreate, and review the childhood movie until we have received the lesson it has to give us and then go on in our lives—as ourselves, able to have healthy, whole, adult relationships.

As you may guess, I subscribe to this kinder view of human nature. I don't believe we're all masochists, but I do believe that it takes us a long time and often many experiences to teach us the things we need to learn about ourselves.

Since adult relationships are our primary means of learning the lessons from childhood, it follows that often these adult relationships will not be the perfectly crystalline, boundlessly happy eternal unions we wish they would be. Rather, it is in their very raggedness, incompleteness, and frustration that they become powerfully instructive. It also follows that through them and at the end of them there will be much to be learned about our relationships with our parents—about what I call the unfinished business of childhood—and hence about ourselves.

For every person—married, living with a partner, or single—the paramount task of living is the creation of the self. The reason relationships are so important to us, and the reason their endings are so painful, isn't just that when they are over we miss the company: it is because through them we undertake the process of bringing ourselves into being.

Let me say again that in my view, it is the creation of the self—living as exactly and wholly as oneself as one possibly can—that is our primary task as human beings. Because relationships assist us in accomplishing this purpose, I see their endings not as tragic but, although needled with pain, as potent opportunities.

4

Charting the Life Span of Love: Seven Relationships and Why They Ended

WHILE IT IS TRUE THAT there are as many variations in relationships and reasons for their endings as there are couples who enter into them, there are also certain basic themes and issues that operate in both the creation and the dissolution of relationships.

What follows are the stories of seven relationships and the issues upon which they foundered and ultimately disintegrated. Although these are composites drawn from among the hundreds of disengaging couples I have seen in therapy, and although no story will exactly replicate your own, I have included them here to provide you with a sort of dictionary of the many kinds of developmental tasks which are consciously or unconsciously undertaken in relationships. They can give you a way of identifying the tasks that are being or have been accomplished in yours.

Because of our obsolete mythologies of love—in particular the myth that love is forever—our natural instinct is to feel as if our relationships have ended "out of the blue," with no real reason whatsoever, or worse yet, for reasons single-handedly precipitated by our spouses or sweethearts. Yet, as these stories reveal, relationships always end for a reason—they end when developmental tasks have been completed by one or both partners.

Rather than being "forever," relationships have lifetimes—they have beginnings and middles and endings. These stories illustrate that fact, and they are presented here to remind you that others, too, have fallen in love, wittingly or unwittingly accomplished their developmental tasks, received the gifts their relationships offered, gone through the process of parting, and, in the end, survived.

Priscilla and Dean: The Norman Rockwell Painting

Dean was the captain of the football team and Priscilla was one of the prettiest girls at the prom. They both went to Ivy League schools and did well enough to be at the top of their respective classes.

When she entered college, Priscilla was unabashedly looking for a handsome, soon-to-be-successful husband from a distinguished family. Dean was on the lookout for a beautiful, intelligent girl who could eventually be the perfect mother for his children and the sparkling hostess at his side. When he met Priscilla at a fraternity party, he recognized at once that she met all his criteria. As for Priscilla, she was totally smitten.

After a proper yearlong engagement, they were married in a vine-covered church the summer she was twenty-one and went to Martha's Vineyard for their honeymoon. After getting his MBA at Harvard (Priscilla worked as a clerk at Filene's to help them out financially), Dean landed a job at a prestigious corporation, and they bought their dream house, a four-bedroom brick colonial with the appropriate white picket fence, a forty-five minute commuter train ride from New York.

Within three years they produced the first of their three stunning children, a girl, who was followed two years later by a second girl, and a year after that by a boy. Weekdays, while Dean was busy climbing the corporate ladder, working late, and pursuing promotions,

Priscilla was packing school lunches, driving her daughters to Girl Scout meetings and ballet lessons, taking her son to Little League practice, helping all three of her children with homework, attending PTA meetings, promoting school plays and carnivals, and generally being the perfect and devoted mother Dean had always expected she would be.

On weekends, as a family they attended football games—their alma maters' and their son's. On Saturdays, Priscilla turned hostess for their perfect dinner parties, and on Sunday mornings, they all went to church.

He was successful; she was the ideal mother and wife; and at the outskirts of the marriage hovered two sets of devoted grandparents. From the outside, at least, theirs was the perfect marriage. In fact, it was not unlike the Norman Rockwell painting of Thanksgiving which hung above the polished Georgian sideboard in their spacious dining room. The children, thanks to Priscilla's devotion, were all high achievers, and one by one, they too went off to Ivy League schools. It was in the quietness that followed that Priscilla began to notice Dean's absence. He was hardly ever home. She had been so occupied with the children—believing their rearing was the expression of what she thought was a mutual purpose—that she had failed to notice Dean's absence or the fact that their emotional paths seldom crossed.

It was when she finally confronted Dean with her feelings of loneliness that she learned he had been punctuating his rise to the top with a long series of affairs. She was devastated by the news. Suspicions she hadn't had the heart to entertain were suddenly being confirmed. Not only had he dropped out of any real participation in their children's lives, but his own emotional life was also being conducted somewhere else. He probably didn't even love her anymore.

After a number of desperate attempts to resurrect their marriage—a change in jobs and geography and several attempts at therapy—their marriage ended painfully, in its thirty-second year.

In time, Priscilla and Dean both came to learn that they had made a marriage to please their parents and their parents' traditions, not a marriage that had any life-stream of its own—and certainly not a marriage in which they had made an emotional partnership with one another. They had both grown up in families that had instructed them to create a marriage that would maintain old family traditions, and they both followed their parents' directives to a tee.

Dean, for example, had been told to marry a mother for his children, not a woman for himself. "Don't be driven by your passions, Dean," his mother had always said. "Pick a good mother for your children, a steady woman, someone who wears well over the years." In a sense, his infidelities were cries for help: "I'm trapped. I'm living out someone else's definition of my life. It doesn't fit."

Meanwhile, Priscilla had become the devoted mother she had never had. She came to realize that because of her unhappy childhood, and a painfully distant relationship with her emotionally withholding mother, she had poured out all her energies on her own children. She also realized that she had chosen a man who, while meeting her family's criteria for good looks and success, really had no desire for emotional closeness with her. In a sense, Dean had been as emotionally distant as her mother.

In Priscilla and Dean's marriage, remarkably enough, the developmental task for each of them had been to grow up, that is, to define themselves as distinct from their parents. Before, and for the most part during their marriage, they had both been incapable of making decisions that truly reflected their own needs as persons. As their marriage disintegrated, these deeper needs and identities emerged;

and it was finally only through the dissolution of their relationship that they declared their independence from their parents' values.

Priscilla and Dean were married in an era in which the traditions and values of the family took precedence over the individual's needs. In a sense, neither one of them had ever been a self. They married before they were able to form their own identities, and the gift from their relationship, painful as it finally was to receive, was the dawning awareness that each of their individual selves had specific content and value and needed to be respected.

Realizing that all of his life he had denied the artistic dimension of his personality, Dean entered graduate school in his fifties, got a master's degree in art, and became a college art professor. After years as an unpaid nurturer, Priscilla finally encountered her long-suppressed interest in finance, and at the age of fifty-six, much to her own surprise, she became a financial counselor. As time passed and they both recovered from the shock of their ended marriage and also attained satisfaction from their new pursuits, they gingerly re-approached one another. Once the dust had settled, it became clear that they both did have a strong concern for their children. After a series of delicate negotiations, they agreed on a plan for mutual guidance of their children, including always getting together as a family on important holidays.

George and Barbara: The Emotional Emergency Room

Barbara was a thirty-six-year-old widow with two children. She had desperately loved her first husband, Nick, who had been a bank vice president. Barbara had had a very difficult childhood, extremely rejecting parents, and, as a result of her father's peripatetic relationship to work, she had endured a great deal of financial hardship. At eighteen she left home, put herself through college, and, at a summer banking job following her graduation, she met Nick, who fell in love with her immediately. They had an intense romantic courtship; by Christmas they were married.

Barbara described her life with Nick as perfect and blissful. "He was the man of my dreams in every way." For the first time in her life she felt both loved and financially secure, and it was with a great sense of joy that after several years she anticipated the birth of the first of their two children. Barbara's life with Nick was so good, in fact, that she felt as if "the spell of my childhood had been broken." As a result of this magical thinking, she was even more devastated than she might otherwise have been when, after nine years of marriage, Nick was killed in a plane crash.

George had been a longtime friend of Nick and Barbara's. He had been a frequent handball partner of Nick's and, in spite of not being married himself, he had for years been included in Nick and Barbara's social circle.

Now thirty-five, George had endured a lifetime of being ignored. He had grown up being virtually invisible in his family, where it had been his role to be "the good child." He had an extremely troublesome older brother who was always creating problems and who, as a result, usurped almost all of his parents' resources and attention. In order to create a role for himself, George had taken on the role of being his mother's confidant and comforter. Being constantly assaulted by her older son's antics and accidents, and feeling abandoned by her husband who "seemed to be working all the time," George's mother needed him—although she never consciously acknowledged this.

For years, George had been doing thoughtful, considerate things that no one, not even his mother, ever identified as valuable. Because no one had ever appreciated his efforts, he had no sense of himself; in fact, he thought he really had nothing to offer anyone.

Encountering Barbara after Nick's death, however, provided the perfect opportunity for him. In her emotionally devastated condition, Barbara saw George as a godsend, "an angel of mercy who arrived exactly when I needed him. I wouldn't have made it without him," she always said. He provided exactly the kind of sensitive care she so desperately needed. George didn't live very far from Barbara, and gradually he started stopping by to see if she and the children were all right. This soon became a ritual, and eventually a sense of expectation became attached to it for both of them. Barbara began to expect his arrival—"I couldn't imagine a day without seeing him"—and he began to look forward to the time they spent together as the high point of his day—"It was like coming home."

It was out of this sensitive nurturing relationship that, quite naturally, their subsequent romance developed. They started going out on dates and within a year they were married. Their marriage, while noticeably lacking in passion and excitement, nevertheless provided a stable healing for Barbara and her two children. Barbara thought she was happy—her most critical needs were certainly being fulfilled—but as she said, "There was also a vague sense of unreality about it all."

Initially, George was happy too. For the first time in his life, what he had to offer was being valued. He started to have a sense of himself. Yet in the background—just as when he was a child—was the feeling that he was really only compensating for someone else's absence. Shortly after their marriage, their relationship began subtly to go downhill.

Before George came along, Barbara had been afraid that she'd never get married again, that after Nick's death she would never love again. She was also afraid, in spite of Nick's financial provisions, that she wouldn't be able to provide for herself and her children, and this had been an underlying motivation in her connecting with George.

Once she was married to George, however, these issues receded, and Barbara's secondary needs began to surface. Having been once again provided with security, she now discovered she had some ambitions she had suppressed during her season of grieving, and she wanted to pursue them. She remembered, for example, that during her first marriage she had wanted to get a nursing degree.

A similar change was occurring for George. Having finally been appreciated for his savior skills, he wanted to unearth his other capabilities. He now felt good enough about himself to ask for support for his own endeavors. He wanted to go into business for himself. Now that Barbara was back on her feet, he hoped she would stand by his side while, based on his newly acquired self-confidence, he made his dream a reality.

Unfortunately, Barbara had no desire to do that. She had needed George to be her helpmate in a dark, disastrous time, to be a rock to which she could cling while she recovered from the devastating setbacks of Nick's death. But now that her recovery was complete, she had no desire whatsoever to play a supporting role for him. She was ready to take off in the direction she had set out for herself before Nick died. She felt so good she couldn't understand why George was so upset—he'd wanted to be her hero, hadn't he? Why was he now discontent?

But now that George had completed the developmental task of learning that what he had to offer was of value, he was ready for what came next on his own interior psychological agenda, namely, learning to receive support for himself. When he revealed his aspirations to Barbara and found that rather than wanting to support him, she had some aspirations of her own, he took his newly found strength, started his own computer firm, and soon announced that he wanted a divorce. Within a year he found a woman who was so impressed by his initiative that she was delighted to play the supporting role in his life.

Was Barbara and George's relationship a failure? No, it was a completion and a new beginning for both of them. As a result of it, Barbara recovered from the devastation of Nick's death and took steps to support herself. In time, she finished nursing school and eventually remarried. For George, it was the circumstance in which he grew beyond serving as an emotional life support system for others and learned how to become a receiver himself.

Neither Barbara nor George had recognized that marriage is not a rescue operation, it is a relationship which must have a raison d'être and a life of its own. It must have substance, content, and validity in and of itself to make it a viable union. In a sense, for Barbara and George, the courtship had been their real relationship. In it, they had given one another the remarkable experience of giving and receiving exactly what they needed at the time. Once they were married, however, those needs subsided and their differences came to the surface, revealing that together they didn't have enough substance for a long-term marriage.

The ending of this relationship was surprisingly efficient. It was also marked by extraordinary good will as George and Barbara both readily acknowledged the ultimate inappropriateness of their union. With touching gratitude they both expressed appreciation for the gifts they had received. Barbara had recovered from her emotional trauma and economic upheaval, and by helping her, George had been able not only to identify but also to take possession of his true strengths and resources as a person. With not too many tears and a real sense of thanksgiving, they went their separate ways; to this day they remain the best of friends.

ed and Laura: The Long Apprenticeship

Ted was an established director living in New York, and Laura was an aspiring actress. They met at a summer theater workshop where for a number of years Ted had been conducting master classes. Ted had already had a series of relationships, each of which had been satisfying to him but now, at almost forty, he was ready to get married. "I wanted the steady footing and deeper commitment I thought a marriage would provide. As a married man, I thought I could focus my energies even more pointedly on directing."

Although most of his earlier partners had been in the arts—a dancer and choreographer, a painter, a graphic artist, and an editor— he had always believed that the perfect mate for him would be one who shared his interest in the theater. He also believed that having done as much "research" as he had, he could now identify the woman who would be physically, intellectually, emotionally, and sexually compatible with him.

He was certainly smitten when he encountered Laura at the workshop. Physically she possessed the Rubensesque voluptuousness he had always preferred, and intellectually she also seemed to be his counterpart. She was well read and seemed willing to have a conversation on almost any subject, and she was obviously a gifted though not yet accomplished actress. Somewhat to his own surprise, he realized that he liked the idea of helping to foster her talent.

Laura saw Ted as "distinguished, dynamic, and successful—a pro who could show me the ropes in the tough theatrical world." His professional stature was a great comfort to her, for although she was deeply committed to being an actress, she harbored the fear that without someone's help she might not make it.

After their initial summer meeting, their careers seemed to throw them together repeatedly. Eventually, they discovered that sexually they were a dynamite match and intellectually they were also great companions. After several months of courtship on the road and another few months of living together, they were married.

They bought a house in Connecticut and settled down. Ted expanded his work as a director, and under his firm-handed guidance and forceful direction, Laura established her acting career. For a dozen years their careers progressed along what seemed to be complementary paths, and in spite of her own emerging and increasingly demanding career, Laura continued, somewhat unthinkingly, to play a supporting role to Ted.

As Laura approached forty, however, she realized she hadn't performed the number and kinds of roles that were critical for her if her career were ever to be firmly established, and she decided to make a firmer commitment to her work.

Insofar as she had already been successful and had been "on the road," Ted had gone through a lot of emotional disappointment and distress. He missed her desperately. While consciously fostering her artistic development, he had unconsciously relied on her to be his "wife," and he wasn't happy at all when, as a result of his masterful tutelage, she started behaving more and more like an actress. At precisely the point where he began to seriously miss her, she began feeling even more strongly that she had to take some further actions to beef up her career.

When Laura's intentions surfaced, Ted became threatened and indignant. He'd made his place in the world; he wanted to settle down and enjoy it—with her. It was time, he thought, for her to set her career aside (it had never amounted to that much anyway) and enjoy the life that his success had created for the two of them. In a surprise dramatic move, he bought a huge new house in Bel Air, which he hoped they would retire to for a second honeymoon.

Instead of loving the house, Laura felt trapped by it. Domestic life was irrelevant to her. Her focus was acting. She felt her time was running out, and she was afraid she'd grow old without ever making her mark in the theater world.

In a dramatic move of her own, she auditioned for a role that would take her on the road for six months. When she got it, Ted exploded. His playmate and ego-support had been taken away, and he felt abandoned by her "self-indulgent" move. It was all right for Laura to have a profession of her own so long as she also continued to function as a wife. But when her career assumed the priority role she was now giving it, Ted was no longer willing to support it.

As Laura needed him less in his role as her mentor and gradually withdrew her doting admiration and support, Ted became abusive. He was constantly angry; he became insulting and demanding. He hit her a number of times. He complained about all the things she had formerly done and was now no longer doing. Laura reacted to his aggression, insults, and discontent by feeling rejected and angry herself until, after many months of arguing, they both began to wonder what they had ever seen in each other in the first place. A series of fights and crises followed that eventually resulted in the dissolution of their marriage.

Ted and Laura had, in fact, completed the developmental tasks they had undertaken together; it was time to move on. Without any conscious awareness, they had married one another for very important reasons. One of Laura's developmental tasks had been external and obvious, to establish her career. With Ted's help, she had attained her goal of becoming a well-respected working actress. But Laura also had a hidden developmental agenda. Though she had chosen to have a career instead of children, she also had a need to express her maternal, compassionate self. Ted's masked insecurity gave her the perfect opportunity. Through his intense need for companionship, she fulfilled her need to nurture by admiring and adoring him.

Ted, who functioned in the mentor role, had a need to be the dominant person in every relationship, to always be the person around whom everything focused. Abandoned by a career-oriented mother at age three, he desperately needed to feel his own value, which he did in the world by being an accomplished director and in his marriage by imparting his knowledge to Laura. He got the gratification of knowing that she needed him, of being the expert upon whom she relied. In return for his efforts, he received her admiration and devotion.

When their relationship ended, Laura had completed the developmental task of establishing her nurturing instincts. Now she was ready to move herself into the life stage where her career would be the predominant focus. For Ted, the conclusion of the relationship did not necessarily mark the completion of his developmental task. He hadn't fully outgrown his hidden dependency needs. He would either find another woman to indulge his ego or he would have had to be willing to take the gift of Laura's nurturing, incorporate it into his self-image, and apply it in the future to a more democratic relationship.

Bill and Rosie: Nobody Else Would Want Me

Bill had been abandoned by his mother at a very early age. She'd been a small-time traveling showgirl and a big time alcoholic, and Bill's arrival on her scene was not at all a happy event. She wasn't even sure, in fact, exactly where he'd come from, but she was certainly sure she'd just as soon he'd go back to wherever that was. He cramped her style, and so when he was thirteen months old it was easy as pie for her to turn him over to her brother and his wife, who lived on a farm in Ohio.

Growing up, Bill liked life with his aunt and uncle. He especially liked his uncle, who had always wanted a son and was delighted with Bill since he and his wife had never been able to produce an heir. Unfortunately, his enthusiasm over the little boy was so great that his wife, Bill's aunt, began to envy him. "You only care about that boy; you don't care a cracker about me," she complained. In time, she developed a series of ailments which made it "necessary" for her to stop caring for little Bill, and at the age of six he was shipped off to the first of the dozens of foster homes where he learned "how to expect the worst and hope for nothing."

At eighteen, he joined the Marines. When he got out, after finding a job in a tree-trimming business, Bill moved in with a fellow from work who said jokingly, "You can be my roommate, but only if you promise to take my ugly sister out on a date."

Rosie, Bill's roommate's sister, certainly wasn't the prettiest girl in the world. In fact, at age twenty, she'd never been out on a date. But like many another "plain" girl, she had compensated for her deficit by developing her personality. She was thoughtful, loving, and kind. She also had a keen intelligence that Bill admired.

Rosie's pitiful homeliness had already been a lifelong sorrow to her. She had been mercilessly criticized by her mother, whose inflated ego couldn't bear the uncomplimentary reflection of her daughter's homeliness. Instead of admiring Rosie for the many capabilities she did, in fact, possess, her mother harped on her about her awful looks, her gracelessness, her lack of "good enough" manners, and her abominable taste in clothes. Her mother reminded her as often as she could that it was a good thing she had a brain because she'd certainly never have a husband.

When Bill asked Rosie out to the movies, she was amazed. "I was dumbstruck. I didn't know how to behave. I guess I'd started believing my mother. I thought I'd never go out on a date." What was even more amazing was that Rosie and Bill discovered they had a lot in common. In their respective isolations they had both become bookworms and had read a lot of the same books. They also had an extraordinary love of nature, and, because of the disappointments of their childhoods, they both had a strong desire to have children.

Rosie was so delighted to have a man in her life that in little unexpected ways she began to perceive herself as worthy—not as pretty, necessarily, but in some way worthy of a man.

On the other hand, Bill was so relieved that finally there was someone to accept him and not pass him off to someone else that his appreciation of Rosie came very quickly to obscure the issue of her homeliness. After a very brief courtship, Rosie and Bill were married.

Rosie got a job as a secretary and Bill continued to work at the landscape company where he had first met Rosie's brother. Within a year—with financial help from her mother—they managed to buy a house, and two years later their first child, a girl, was born. Rosie stopped working to stay at home with the baby; two years later twin sons were born.

Because Rosie cared for him and was so grateful that he had chosen her, Bill eventually developed enough self-confidence to try for a job he really wanted. It was also because of her appreciation for him that he was able to keep that job and subsequent ones for a considerable length of time. This was shocking to him since, if anything, his vocational history had taught him that wherever he was, he wouldn't be there long.

Rosie also gained a certain feeling of worth from her marriage. She finally felt like a woman. In the same way she was grateful to Bill for validating her, she was also grateful to her children. They conferred a distinctly feminine identity on her; in response, she doted on them.

In stunning contrast to the expectations generated by their histories, both of them felt that their days as outcasts were over. Finally they were sharing in the common human experience.

Over time, though, Rosie became increasingly focused on her children and spent long hours at home with them. She started to drink. When she drank, for some reason she couldn't define, she felt Bill didn't really care anymore about her or the children. In a myriad of little ways she started to sabotage the relationship. She accused Bill of flirting with other women at parties and finally of having affairs. When drunk, she became so obsessed with these thoughts that her accusations and Bill's denials became virtually the only content of their relationship. Eventually, she destroyed all the sweetness in their life. For as Bill started feeling more and more emotionally abandoned and scared about Rosie's drinking, he finally did have an affair. When, after months of merciless accusations hauntingly reminiscent of her mother, he finally admitted it, Rosie went off on a binge. Bill realized she had a serious drinking problem and that without knowing it he had married an incipient alcoholic. After repeatedly pleading with her to get help, he realized she wasn't ready to change and he filed for divorce.

The developmental tasks in this relationship for both Bill and Rosie had to do with developing a sense of self-esteem. Although she didn't complete the process with him, Rosie did make some progress in repairing her shredded self-esteem and was able to take possession of at least a portion of her feminine identity. Through her marriage to Bill, she incorporated three other beings into her life. For a time she was able to love them and to receive their love in return. Had it not been for her sabotage through alcohol, she might have left the relationship with much more self-esteem than when she entered it.

For Bill, the marriage was a time of healing, and its ending was a wound. His developmental task had been to feel he was worthy of belonging, that he was a valuable enough person to have a home and family, and he had felt that for a time.

In spite of Bill's adoration and appreciation for her, Rosie was unable to use their relationship to completely heal her wounded self-esteem. No matter how much he praised her, no matter how much he enjoyed her, Rosie's convictions about her ugliness could never be erased. As Bill became more and more comfortable with himself in the outside world and he ventured with increasing confidence farther and farther out into it, Rosie began to feel inadequate again. As he made a place for himself in a world she believed she was too homely to inhabit, she felt her only possible role in life was as a mother; consequently, she withdrew her love from him and focused on the children, and eventually on her drinking. She created a fantasy of his affairs to support her long-held theory of her basic unworthiness, and because she would not be swayed from it, in time it became a self-fulfilling prophecy. Rosie left Bill convinced that her mother was right—it was a miracle she'd ever had a husband.

After therapy, Bill recognized that he had married a person with a drinking problem just like his mother. Along with understanding this tragic similarity, he was also able to reconnect with all the good things he had gained in his marriage to Rosie. He realized that Rosie's inability to accept herself was really her problem, that he had truly loved her and fully intended to share his whole life with her. Along the way, his self-esteem had been enhanced. He had completed his developmental task: he felt acceptable as a human being. At thirty-eight he enrolled as a college freshman and felt as if miraculously a new world had opened to him.

Rosie didn't fare as well. Instead of using Bill's gifts to continue to develop her self-esteem, Rosie reverted to her mother's negating opinion of herself. She refused to receive the gifts of her relationship.

Instead of allowing it to enlarge her, she ended it in bitterness and without the benefit of healing insight.

Tom and Margaret: The Second Adolescence

Margaret, a financially independent real estate agent, had spent most of her life being a caretaker to others. Her mother had had, as Margaret always said, "the audacity to die when I was ten," and Margaret became the surrogate parent to six younger brothers and sisters. As an adult, she had put her husband through graduate school and then herself through training as a radiological technician. During her forties, she switched to real estate, and came to the time in her life when, according to her, "it was my turn to have an adolescence."

At this point, she became involved with Tom, a man in his late twenties. Tom, blond, athletic, and very attractive, was the child of wealthy, self-indulgent parents. Margaret was wildly flattered that he was even interested in her. When he shamelessly pursued her, she found him irresistible.

Tom was a surfer who specialized in having fun. He was an expert on play. He knew a million ways to relax and he was willing to teach them all to her. He took her dancing, roller-skating, hiking, and canoeing. He surprised her with flowers and candy and played with her at the beach. Having caught the stride of his carefree example, when Margaret won a prize for real estate sales, she took him on a trip to Egypt.

They were concerned about the difference in age. "I'm probably having an affair with my mother," Tom said, but the truth is that in their relationship, Margaret was more like a father to Tom. Because she had taken up the burdens of responsibility so long ago and had functioned for years so efficiently in the world, she was very accomplished at what in our culture are traditionally male roles. She was a very directed person. She knew the importance of work, of having goals, and planning for the future, while Tom, whose parents had never given him guidance on how to proceed toward his goals, was completely unfocused.

While Margaret was teaching Tom to grow up, Tom was teaching Margaret, as she always said, to grow down. "It never occurred to me that part of my life could be spent having fun. 'Life equals work'—that was my motto. But Tom taught me how to play—more important, he showed me the value of play. I'd always thought play was a waste, but Tom made it legitimate. At fifty-four, I finally had an adolescence; I finally learned to waste time."

If Margaret was so happy, then why did their playful relationship end? Like any other adolescent who has had a satisfying time of irresponsibility, Margaret was eventually eager to move on to all the expansive possibilities of grown-up life. "One day I just started feeling as if I'd had enough," she said. "I was ready to get on with things. I realized I was about to get involved in international real estate and I couldn't be sitting at the beach all day. I also had to face a significant—and truly unrealistic—age difference between us. The thought of my being sixty—I was already starting to see the signs of my aging in all-too-graphic ways—and his still being in his twenties was too awful; I knew I couldn't handle it."

Tom was the reluctant finisher in this relationship. His grasp on his own childhood was still a bit shaky when Margaret decided to end it. As he said, "Who wants to grow up? I could have kept playing for years." It was in their parting, though, that he received the richest legacy of their relationship. "When Margaret left me, I had no choice; I had to grow up, and I discovered that because of the time I'd spent with her, I actually could. I'd always wanted to be a lawyer; and since Margaret had always made work seem so easy, I was finally willing to invest the same time and energy and discipline I knew it would take. Before I met Margaret, I'd never imagined that I could be successful. It was devastating, terrible when she broke up with me, but in the long run it was for the best."

Tom and Margaret's relationship filled a developmental gap in each of their histories. Tom learned that work could be an important and positive part of his life; and Margaret was finally able to experience the playful interlude she missed because of having had her adulthood forced upon her so early.

The age discrepancy between Tom and Margaret exemplifies a reversal of what has occurred between older men and younger women for years. It is only now, with the new freedoms available to women, that the older woman/younger man scenario is more visible. But no matter what the sex of the older partner in such a relationship, the developmental task for that person is usually to experience a part of life that was previously rushed or missed entirely.

Sharon and Harold: The Professional Corporation

Sharon and Harold met while they were finishing their graduate degrees in architecture at UCLA. They were both highly innovative and ambitious designers; however, neither one was ready to work for a big architectural firm nor to strike out alone. They decided to pool their resources and set up a business together, one in which they would share the risks of starting out in a highly competitive profession. It was the emotional involvement required by their joint enterprise that eventually blossomed into romance.

"In the beginning, I wasn't really sexually attracted to Harold," Sharon said later, "but as we started working together and I realized all the good things that were happening for me because I had allied myself with him, I gradually started feeling attracted to him. I realized he had what I needed—initiative and guts. His energy inspired me, and in the end it was knowing that he could help me achieve my professional goals that made him irresistible to me."

Since Sharon and Harold had each been married before and neither had any children, they decided that this time, instead of getting married, they would live together. They wanted a different format for their new relationship. They did, however, decide to buy a warehouse together, which they renovated to serve as both living quarters and an office.

The first year or two of their relationship they put all their time and energy into revamping the warehouse and pursuing every business lead that came along. They were often exhausted; at times they were near the edge financially, and Harold's temper got short. But after a year and a half, the warehouse was finished, business picked up, and their relationship smoothed out. They celebrated their second anniversary and their firm's first sizable commission by taking a honeymoon trip to Mexico.

As time went on, they got more clients and their reputation spread—or, to be more precise, Sharon's reputation spread. Sharon, it seemed, had a special touch with design, a flourish of imagination, and sensitivity to her clients that it became increasingly clear Harold lacked.

As time went on, Harold could no longer handle his anger about Sharon's success, and he started letting it out in their personal life. He began by condescendingly picking on her. He maligned her appearance, her habits, her friends, and he progressed eventually to putting her down by having a series of blatant affairs. They had more and more fights over his shabby treatment of her, until finally arguments were their only form of contact. After many months in therapy struggling over the painful issues of her self-worth, Sharon unilaterally ended the relationship.

"I suppose," said Harold, "I hadn't really expected she would have more clients than me. In some sense, even though we were partners and even though I wanted us to be equal, I couldn't handle it when I realized that she was more talented. She was doing the kind of designs I'd always hoped I'd be able to do. Deep down I'd always expected that I'd be in the lead, that she'd play, at least to the tiniest degree, a slightly supporting role. I just couldn't face the fact that in the long run she's probably going to be more successful than me. I thought I was a liberated man, but I'm not. And that's the bottom line. That's why I got involved with other women, I suppose. I needed to feel superior to someone."

In the beginning of their relationship, Sharon and Harold were at a similar point in their developmental process. They were both attempting to achieve a particular goal they had already identified. But one of the unconscious motivators for most successful and ambitious people is competition. It is the desire not only to succeed, but also to be a whole lot better than one's peers that fuels the first achievement. In a partnership such as Harold and Sharon's, the matter of competition remained submerged until, through changing circumstances, it became apparent that in the pursuit of their goals they were not exactly equals. Sharon's capabilities somewhat exceeded Harold's, and when he sensed this, his own inherent competitive instincts were activated, causing him to perceive Sharon no longer as a colleague but as a competitor. The continuation of their relationship was eroded by the emergence of the awful truth that, in fact, she was a much better architect than he.

Harold's infidelities were his way of getting out of what had become for him an untenable situation. After Sharon kicked him out of the house, he reestablished his business in another town where, without having his abilities continually compared to hers, he was happy in his work.

From their relationship, Harold learned that he worked much better alone than in a partnership. His experience with Sharon also taught him the ropes of beginning a business so that later, when he had to do it on his own, he was able to do it without fear.

Harold's confidence in Sharon and his initial willingness to enter into a partnership with her were his gifts to her. He provided her with companionship and a professional buffer as she made the transition from student to established professional. Having established herself in what was soon a very successful career, Sharon's next developmental task was to give attention to deepening her emotional life. After numerous exploratory relationships—many of which repeated the threatened response she had experienced with Harold—she fell in love with and married one of her clients, an eminent physician who was not at all threatened by her success.

Sharon and Harold exemplify the dual career relationship that is a frequent modern phenomenon. As both men and women explore the limits of their creativity and personal development, Sharon and Harold's problems, which centered on issues of competition and sex roles, are becoming increasingly familiar.

Liz and Mike: Nothing but Sex

Liz, in her late twenties, was a knockout and knew it. Thirty-five-year-old Mike was also a knockout, but that didn't matter to him. What mattered was that he liked his work as an insurance salesman and aside from work, his sex life was the only thing he cared about.

"It's very simple," he said. "For me, after work, sex is number one. I don't want fame. I don't want to travel all over the world. I don't need cars and houses to impress my friends. I like my work, but what matters to me after that is . . . sex."

"Before I met Mike," Liz said, "I wasn't even sure I really liked sex. Most of my sexual experiences had been lukewarm. I married my high school sweetheart and we had a daughter immediately. Our sex life got lost somewhere along the way. But after my divorce, when I got involved with Mike, I started to realize how important sex really is to me. It was like opening a door. At times I felt really weird, like I'd become a nymphomaniac or something.

"I had this incredible sex with him, unlike anything I'd ever experienced, and since the sex was so fantastic, I figured I must be in love. When he asked me to marry him four months into our relationship, of course I agreed. I felt I couldn't live without him. It never occurred to me to think of what it would be like when we actually started living together, how we'd both feel with my daughter around, how he would feel after giving up his apartment. Mike had never been married. I think he thought of our marriage—and I guess I did too—as just a continuation of our incredible sex life."

It wasn't like that, of course. Real life impinged. There were all the usual domestic difficulties: plumbing that broke, a child with homework to do, trash to be taken out, bills to be paid. Not only were all these obligations unpleasant in themselves, but they also severely hampered the kind and amount of incredible sex that, up until their impulsive marriage, had been the main event of their every encounter.

Mike found in time that the very arrangement he had entered into in hopes of securing a steady stream of mind-boggling sex had backfired on him. He had much less sex and a houseful of domestic obligations. From time to time, he was tempted to leave, but the memory of and the anticipation of more mind-boggling sex kept him tied to the relationship. As long as their relationship was focused on sex and avoided the issues of real life—her child, their finances, the future—it worked like a charm.

But as time passed, it became more and more apparent that, aside from sex, Liz and Mike had very little in common. Their relationship dwindled into trivial daily exchanges. From time to time, they would make half-hearted attempts to do something different—take a vacation, join a health club together, or create a social life—but nothing really worked.

When they came to me to identify the underlying emotional issues in their relationship, it became clear that for both of them sex carried many more meanings than the physical satisfaction it so reliably provided. For Liz, it represented the years of physical nurturing she had never received as a child. Her mother had had tuberculosis when Liz was young, and as a result, she had been unable to hold Liz for years. Psychologically, Liz was a little girl whose body was starved for affection.

For Mike, sex was an experience of power. As a child, his personal power had always been challenged and denigrated by his father. Because his father had been too shy to talk about sex, it became the only expression of Mike's power that hadn't been tampered with. In addition, his mother had been "an iceberg," and he felt as if he too had grown up without any physical affection. "It's as if I'm a thousand years behind in the physical contact department," he said.

Understanding the deeper meanings behind their physical relationship allowed Liz and Mike to realize that sex really was the only thing they had in common. They were both making up for some painful deficiencies from childhood; at the same time, they used sex as a defense mechanism to stave off the responsibilities of further growth.

Their gift to each other was that they really did heal some painful old wounds from their childhoods. Their sexual bonding had the effect of fulfilling some deep-seated needs for physical affection. They were finally able to identify that part of their developmental process as complete, to move on in their lives, to incorporate other interests, and to identify their true individual priorities.

Following her sexual renaissance, Liz decided she needed to spend more quality time with her daughter—that parenting had become a real priority for her. She hoped to find a man who would happily assume the role of surrogate father as well as be a more comfortable mate for herself.

Following his sortie into family life, Mike realized that he really preferred to live alone, that he definitely didn't like playing the role of a father, and that he needed to develop some other interests besides work and sex. After a four-month courtship and a little more than a year of marriage, Mike and Liz were divorced.

As Liz and Mike's relationship shows, sex in itself, no matter how extraordinarily compelling, is not enough to sustain a relationship. Although it may be the magnet which draws two people together, unless it is part of a much larger sphere of commonality, it too will eventually become uninteresting and the relationship it was meant to sustain will ultimately collapse.

As these seven relationships show, despite the pain of parting, relationships always have good, legitimate, and even necessary reasons for coming to an end, and their endings invariably coincide with the completion of developmental tasks.

All human beings are pointed toward growth and expansion. Relationships are, for each of us, the most profound vehicle for personal development. Self-creation is a continual forward-moving process, and either intuitively or consciously, we all gravitate toward those persons who can assist us in our process. In the same fashion, when a given step in our process has been completed, we find ourselves consciously or unconsciously testing the limits of our relationships to see if our present partners will be the appropriate allies for forthcoming stages in our personal development.

However, because of the old assumption that only forever counts, we have not been able to think of the endings as signs that a cycle has been completed. Instead, we have tended to assume that the endings in themselves were bad. The truth is that although endings always involve pain, whatever comes into our lives and transforms us is to be celebrated. We don't curse the person who brings us a bouquet of flowers because a few days later the flowers wilt and we have to throw them away. We celebrate the gift and think it is appropriate to say thank you. We're glad to have had a chance to enjoy the bouquet for as long as it lasted.

In just the same way, we need to start thinking of relationships as having lifetimes, lifetimes that come to an end in their own due season. We need to revamp the myth that implies that the only valid relationship is the one we take with us to the grave.

We also need to be thankful. Whenever a relationship is given to us, we need to be grateful and rejoice. Even when a relationship ends, we should celebrate the fact that something has been exchanged that has been of value to both people. When we come to the end of our journey together, we should acknowledge that we are being delivered to the next place in our lives much more safe or whole, more at ease, or more expanded and complete as persons than we were when we entered the relationship. The selves who made the union are in much better condition at its end, even though the suffering and confusion of the ending often make this difficult to see.

If we look only at the relationship, then we must grieve; but if we look at the individuals who loved one another, then we can celebrate. Along with saying that the relationship has ended—something is gone—we should tell ourselves that something wonderful has been accomplished. What we have at the end of a relationship is two transformed human beings, people who have changed so much that they are now ready for the next miraculous stage of their personal development.

5

The Emotional Process of Parting

THERE ARE MANY STAGES of ending a relationship. No relationship ends "out of the blue" even though many of us think they do. An ending is arrived at by a multitude of increments, by many episodes of discontent, by many conflicts and breakdowns in communication, by many unresolvable disappointments and disillusionments. The coming apart of a relationship, just like the establishment of one, is a complex and intricate process.

In its emotional dimensions, the ending of a relationship has certain similarities to the process we go through when we are grieving a death. There is, however, one important difference. When someone has died, we enter into a grief process that goes through many states and ultimately reaches a resolution. As we go through all these stages, there is always the underlying recognition that the person being mourned is dead. Although with a death there are many stages of grief, of wishing otherwise, of hoping and praying for a miracle, the mourner is always confronted by the incontrovertible fact that someone has died and no change of mind or circumstance will ever bring that person back.

One of the reasons, by the way, that I am not dealing here with relationships that end because of the death of one of the partners is that the emotional issues are different. When a relationship ends because of a death, there is no going back; there is no chance to consider the possibilities of reinstating it. When a death has occurred, emotional resolution must be achieved because the survivor must come to the acceptance that the relationship is over and nothing can change that fact.

When a relationship ends voluntarily, however, and the person with whom one has made that relationship continues to be alive somewhere, perhaps even married to somebody else or still waiting around heartbroken, there is always—in our minds at least—the possibility of reviving the relationship. "Maybe we should try again" is the poignant theme of many a person in the final stages of ending a relationship, and it is often a postscript feeling a year or, tragically, several years later for many people who have already ended their relationships. It is also a feeling that, when acted upon, can result in huge amounts of wasted time.

It's because we so often don't understand what was really going on in our relationships, what was being transacted at an unconscious level, that we go through so many layers of doubts, so many episodes of confusion and regret, so many returns to the scene of the crime, when our relationships end. Because we haven't clearly identified what brought us together in the first place and what we were, in fact, accomplishing in our relationships, we have no idea whatsoever whether or not it is appropriate for them to end—hence, the welter of desperate, confused, and confusing feelings.

Just as there are a set of clearly identified feelings that mark the grief-for-dying process, so there are also a series of clearly identifiable stages of feeling that people go through as they process the ending of a relationship. This set of feelings always applies, whether the relationship was a thirty-two-year marriage, a four-year living-together relationship, a yearlong romance, or a relationship as seemingly inconsequential as a three-week affair.

In fact, in some ways, the pain of ending a brief romance seems more exquisite than the pain of ending a long-term relationship. The reason for this, I believe, is that in a long-term relationship, partners know both sides of the coin, the imperfections as well as the pleasures of a relationship with this particular partner, while in a brief romance, there is usually still boundless hope.

While the charting of these emotional stages typifies the order in which most people go through their emotional process, it is also true that any of these stages may occur in a slightly, or even very, different order, and any one of these feeling stages may be repeated one or even many times.

The ending of a relationship creates a wound that must be healed, and it follows that in order to complete the process of healing, we may go through a given feeling or set of feelings numerous times. Healing doesn't happen overnight. For example, you may go through the stage of feeling your own guilt ("It's all my fault") and feel that as a result you have arrived at a different emotional place, only to find that some event or memory reignites the feeling, causing you to go back and feel your way through it once again.

The process of change—of emotional resolution—requires many experiences of the feeling that is being resolved until, through repetition, resolution finally occurs. These repetitions may take weeks, they may be completed in a single cathartic day, or they may recur, first subliminally and then consciously, over many years.

You will find—especially if you are still at the stage of wondering whether or not your relationship is ending or should end—that you may have already been through some or most of these feelings to some limited degree, even if you have subsequently set them aside because of your fear or because of the pressing contingencies of life. In that case, this brief catalogue will serve to identify feelings that will very likely repeat themselves in the future, until you resolve the conflicts within your relationship or realize that they are irreconcilable.

If you are already in the process of ending a relationship, you will probably notice that you have been through one or several of these feeling stages more than once, probably even a number of times. Don't despair. Certain points of passage in the process of parting are harder to go through than others and need to be repeated more often.

The purpose of the charting that follows is to give you an opportunity to validate the emotional experience you are having right now, to give you a sense of what is likely to come after what you are experiencing now, to let you know that the feelings you are having are appropriate, and to tell you that along with the multitude of others who have already gone through the process of parting, you too will survive.

I Can't Believe This Is Happening to Me

Invariably the first feeling that accompanies any awareness that a relationship is ending is, "I can't believe this is happening to me." At the very moment the unacceptable information is being admitted to your consciousness, there is an instant attempt at denial. On the one hand, you are saying, "I know this is happening to me," and at the very same time you are saying, "I can't stand it and, therefore, I don't want to believe that this is, in fact, what's happening to me."

All the interior statements that support the position that this really can't be happening dredge up from the deeper layers of consciousness: "This marriage was made in heaven. We were going to sit out our old age together in our rocking chairs." "We were the perfect match; we've had so many really good times." "It can't be true, it isn't true, it just can't possibly be true that he's been having an affair, that he just doesn't love me anymore."

"This isn't happening. This can't be happening to me. To us! Why, only last week we had a fantastic vacation together. Why, only last summer our friends were calling us the perfect couple."

"Not us! We had the perfect romance. Everybody said so. No! Not us! My God, we were just planning our wedding, picking out china and crystal. This can't be happening to us."

"This certainly can't be happening to me. Not me! Bad things aren't supposed to happen to me. I've always led a charmed life. Well, maybe not a charmed life. But certainly an okay life, a happy life. Not painful like this. Not devastating like this. Not wracked with surprises like this. This can't be happening to me."

"This can't be happening to me. Other people break up. Other people's marriages end after thirty-two years, not mine. Other people's dreams get nipped in the bud, not mine. Other people get rejected, not me."

Another form of "This can't be happening to me" is, "I can't be doing this. I can't be ending my marriage. I can't be walking away from all this—from my wife, my house, and my kids. This isn't me. I can't be doing this. Other people are cruel and crass and mean and selfish enough to walk out on their marriages. Not me. I'm a nice person. I wouldn't just walk out on someone. I wouldn't have an affair. I did, though. But I'm not that kind of person. Not really. And I meant it when I married her—in sickness and in health. Forever. Till death do us part and all that jazz. I can't be doing this."

This first recognition that a relationship is ending brings up a thousand versions of denial. That a relationship about which you posited a forever is ending is unthinkable; the one thing you thought would never happen in your life is happening.

Directly, consciously for the first time, you are facing the fact that, oh, my God, yes, this really is happening to me. Immediately on the heels of that recognition—almost like the Red Cross arriving with a stretcher and some tourniquets—a great array of denials rushes in so the patient doesn't die of shock.

Sometimes even this denial takes an unconscious form. As one person said, "When Rick first said he was leaving me, it was a physical sensation. It was as if the whole world, my body and life itself had ceased to exist."

Many people find themselves unable to eat, to carry on a normal relationship with their bodies. "I've lost ten pounds since David told me it was over," or, "I haven't slept for days. I can't believe this is happening to me."

"I can't stop drinking; I've smoked four thousand cigarettes. I'm killing myself, but I don't care. I can't believe that this is happening to me."

"I can't stop shaking. I can't eat and I can't stop shaking. I just can't believe that this is happening to me."

All these people are expressing emotions, intellectual perceptions, and physical feelings that are way beyond their normal range of experience. What the intensity and strangeness of these feelings indicate is that in our emotional repertoire we have no precedents for the feelings that the endings of relationships arouse in us. Since we do assign to our relationships the meaning and the expectation that they will be invincible and last forever, that we will never have to go through the terrible range of feelings we are going through now, we really don't have an emotional blueprint for ending a relationship. So when we experience these feelings, we feel out of control and terrified. But in spite of their unfamiliarity, these are the natural feelings that constitute the first step in the emotional process of ending a relationship.

You Can't Do This to Me

A more specifically painful form of "This can't be happening to me" occurs when the ending of a relationship marks the completion of a developmental phase for one person, but not for the other. To the other person, the ending feels like a disaster. It feels like the wrong time, the last thing in the world that he or she ever wanted to happen. It feels like a unilateral decision, and the person who is the "victim" of the decision feels devastated and ripped off.

"You can't leave me. The children are too young. You can't leave me to raise them all by myself."

"You can't leave me. I'm not done with school. I'll never be able to finish without you. You promised you'd help, and now you're leaving."

"I'm perfectly happy. You can't leave me. I don't want this, I don't need this, I can't handle this. What's the matter with you? You can't just up and leave me."

"You can't leave me. I'll go crazy. I'll kill myself. I can't live without you. You can't leave me."

"You can't leave me. I can't fail at marriage again. I can't be divorced another time."

"You can't leave me. My parents will never get over it. What will they say? It'll break their hearts. You just can't leave me."

"You can't leave me. I can't live by myself. I can't stand it, being here alone. You just can't leave me. I can't take care of myself."

"You can't leave me. It'll be the end of my career, the end of my business, the end of my reputation, the end of my public image. I can't manage without you. You're not allowed to do this to me."

"You can't leave me. It'll be the end of me financially. Curtains. A disaster. I'll be broke, and you'll lose everything. You're crazy. You can't leave me."

The truth is that any relationship that one person clearly wants to end is a relationship that has outlived its usefulness or come to the end of its life span. If one person doesn't want to be in it to the extent of starting to negotiate the ending, it's clear that there is only one person in that so-called relationship. The relationship is no longer a relationship; it's one person having a fantasy that a relationship exists.

The person who is unilaterally having the fantasy—and that is always the one who says, "I don't see why she had to end it; I was happy; everything seemed perfect to me"—is revealing through those very remarks the fact that there has been an incredible breakdown in the relationship. The person making those statements has obviously not even been aware of the extreme discontent, distancing, or even absence that the other person has been feeling or acting out.

It's always true when a relationship ends that one person plays the role of the instigator to a greater degree than the other. For example, the husband who has had forty-two affairs and walks in after thirty years of marriage and says, "I'm leaving; I've been terribly unhappy and I've been fooling around for fifteen years," is playing the role of the instigator. Yet he isn't bringing this news to a wife who was perfectly happy all those years. The wife who was in that marriage did not have a husband who loved her. Rather, she had a social circumstance that included a man whom she referred to as her husband. Whether she acknowledges it or not, at some level she was experiencing his withdrawal and nonparticipation, even though she may not have been conscious of it. The truth is that she was not—could not have been—in a happy marriage because her husband wasn't there being lovingly married to her.

This is a very important thing for people to know. It is especially important for the person who gets left to understand that at an unconscious level both people are in pretty much the same place about the viability of the relationship. It is also very important to consciously acknowledge this fact. Without this acknowledgment, people who "are left" can very easily begin to think of themselves as victims, as not having participated in the decision that is being leveled against them. In fact, they are participating in it, they have participated in it, and it is a decision that they have consciously or unconsciously also been shaping.

I'll Do Anything, Just Say It Isn't So

After the initial denial of what is occurring, it gradually dawns on us that, in fact, the relationship is ending. Whether the other person has decided to end it—and we see ourselves as the victim in a scenario that was created without so much as a by-your-leave from us—or whether what has finally been articulated strikes us as the inescapable truth—that this really is the swan song of the relationship we thought was going to last forever—there is a feeling of incredible panic.

Denial hasn't worked. Reality is starting to sink in, and panic is the emotion that attends the facing of this terribly uncomfortable reality.

This is true, by the way, for both partners, not only for the one who has had the news of the ending arrive like a bad surprise, but also for the person who has initiated the ending. Although for the initiator the waves of panic may be less frequent and less totally devastating, the panic is real for both partners: "I'll do anything if somehow we can just forget all this and make it go away."

"Can't we please make it all go away? I'll do anything; just make it all go away. Tell me it was just a bad dream. Forget all the things I thought were terrible. Forget I didn't take out the garbage, forget the overdrawn charge accounts, forget the summer vacations you promised and we never took, forget our mediocre sex, forget my mother; forget your mother, forget my ambition, forget my flirting, forget the fact that we never have any fun together anymore or never had any, for that matter; forget that you won't give up Monday Night Football. I'll do anything; just say it isn't so."

"I'll do anything—just say it isn't so. I'll cut my hair or grow my hair. I'll shave my beard or grow a beard. I'll stop drinking. I'll never raise my voice again. I'll stop spending money like a drunken sailor; I will. I'll go out and buy myself some decent underwear. Just tell me what to do. I promise, I'll do anything. Just say it isn't so."

"Forget all my complaints. Forget everything I thought was wrong. I can't face life without you and life without a relationship. I don't care what was the matter. Let's go on a vacation, let's get therapy, let's forget everything—you're perfect. Let's start over."

This is, essentially, a stage of bargaining. There is a desperate, daredevil attempt to rescue, to salvage, to put the genie back in the bottle and say, "No, no, we never said those things to each other," because at this point we are facing for the first time what life would be like without the relationship.

It's also at this point in the process that many people become terrified. Often they have made a passive attempt to end the relationship, for example, by having an affair, but then panic sets in. They go back to the marriage without solving any of its problems, only to have another affair, and end the marriage years later.

Because the feelings at this stage are so terrible, because the panic is so great, we really do feel willing to do anything to put the genie back in the bottle—not because the relationship can be salvaged, but simply because we're scared.

In my experience, very rarely has a relationship gotten to this point and had enough life left in it to be resuscitated. Often panic does lead to reconciliation, but usually to an uneasy truce that results years later in an ending that has only been delayed.

Several people going through the process of ending a relationship have told me about passing through this stage at some time before, and regretting that at the time they hadn't had the courage or received the encouragement to complete the ending of their relationship then. (It may be argued, however, that going through this stage a couple of times makes it easier to finally go through it to the end. Most people say that it does. "I remember feeling this way before," one man said, "and I remember what happened afterward—nothing. That gives me the strength to end it this time.")

There are, of course, those rare instances where coming face to face with the reality that a relationship is ending for all time causes people to finally deal with the issues they have been avoiding. In a few wonderfully exceptional instances, this terrible crisis point has caused people to uncover the strengths in their relationship, to deal with the problems, and to make the creative compromises that allow the relationship to be transformed and, therefore, to survive. This transformation, however, depends on the inherent quality of the relationship, on whether or not it has enough elements to keep it together or to renew it.

"I tried to get divorced six years ago," said Alex, "but then my wife and I went for counseling, and since we weren't biting each other's heads off, it seemed like we ought to stay married. The minute we stopped the counseling, our marriage went flat—or back to flat—where it had already been for years. Finally, I just couldn't stand it anymore, and that's why we're splitting up now. But you know what? I really regret those six years. Nothing good happened between us, and I missed out on a lot of things I'm finally trying now."

"I wanted to get divorced three years ago," said Pam, "but I was chicken. My husband was chicken, too, so after we'd practically murdered each other—I even moved out for a while—we just put everything back in the can and screwed the lid back on and went on with our miserable marriage. Three more years of the pits. But I just didn't have the guts at the time, and neither did he."

When people get to this stage, when they face the devastating reality that the person they've been complaining about, who's been boring them to death, or who's driven them crazy is actually leaving, there is a real feeling of terror. That's often when people come into counseling and say, "Help! Can't we work it out? We'll do anything. We'll spend any amount of money. We'll do anything, try anything. Just say it isn't so."

I'll Never Stop Crying

After the stunned recognition that what you hoped would never happen to you is happening to you, there is the amazed awareness that a profound and gigantic loss is occurring, and it is this recognition which throws people into deep sorrow and grieving.

What rises now to the surface of your consciousness is the awareness that you are losing not only a companion, but also a history, a way of being, a social context, a sense of identity, a blueprint of your future, and, on the most basic level, a definition of yourself.

At this point in the emotional process, you are not particularly interested in getting through the ending or exploring its creative potentials. This is the season for mourning, for bidding a sorrowful, tearful, weeping, and often wailing farewell to all that was, to all that was hoped for, and to all that is no more.

It is now that most people go through a specific, often days-long period of mourning, of deep, almost nonstop crying, accompanied by the feeling of being immobilized by grief.

One woman said, "I thought I would drown in my tears. I couldn't even remember the person I was before the onslaught of all this pain. I seemed to be locked into it, like a bad girl locked in her room, and I really wondered if I would ever go through a day without tears again."

A man said, "In the past few weeks I've cried so much. I've been shaken to the core by this thing, by this change in events, this alteration in plans. The crying is good, but the pain is still there. I'm not over it yet. There must be more tears."

"I've cried for three days straight, nonstop," said someone else. "It's as if everything we had, everything we ever did came back to me all at once, and I had to cry about it all. It was like watching a movie. This is your life. Every tender moment we had ever shared, all the heart-wrenchers, they all came back, and I had to weep for every one of them."

"This is the first day I've come out—I mean, literally left my house. I feel wobbly, but cleansed. The world outside seems strange. Unfamiliar. New. But I'm still feeling very bruised. Not sure that I can survive out here."

Along with the mourning, there is also fear, the feeling that tears are somehow unacceptable, that we ought not to cry. In our culture, we're afraid of depth of feeling, particularly of tears. Our emotional PR to ourselves is that we are better, stronger, and sturdier and will be more happy and successful if we suppress our tears. In a sense, we've told ourselves that it isn't adult—or American—to cry. "I don't know why I'm so upset," one man said, "I just can't seem to get a hold of myself." Or, "I went out to dinner and just started bawling in the restaurant. I feel like a fool. I'm embarrassed; I feel like an idiot. I can't stop crying."

Or, "When is this going to stop? I can't get my work done; I can't get anything done."

"I've been a total wreck, an absolute faucet in front of the kids. What are they going to think, seeing their father falling apart?"

"I've cried myself silly. My friends are getting sick of me. I just can't seem to get it together."

It is a tragedy that at the very moment in the emotional process when the tears are rising up and spilling over, when they insist on coming out, that we have conflict about them. Our hearts and bodies want desperately to cry, to feel the release of our tears, but our mythologies say we should suppress our tears, that we should just "get on with it," that we can't afford the detour for a good hard cry. For all these reasons, when our tears overtake us, we feel weak, unacceptable, and afraid.

Over and over, I see people who have just gone through what has been the most devastating emotional severance of their lives apologizing for their tears. "I'm sorry," they say, reaching for the Kleenex. "Forgive me. Just give me a minute; I'll pull myself together."

This is not the time to pull yourself together. This is the time for more Kleenex and more tears. It's appropriate when you are in sorrow to cry, and the more you cry, the more your sorrow will subside. Although many people fear that their tears will overwhelm them and they'll never stop crying, the truth is that this never happens. Never. The more you cry, the more you facilitate the process of grieving, and the more you facilitate your grieving, the sooner your wounds will heal.

It is only if you have come apart to the depth of your tears, to the depth of your sorrow, to the depth of your hopes and your dreams and your expectations and your memories that you will ever be able to knit yourself back together again.

Your tears are not only important, they are essential. They are the vehicle through which the healing occurs. Welcome them. Respect them. Give them room. And time.

It is essential to honor the tears as a critical part of the healing process, to know that you must go through them in order to get beyond them. I can assure you that you won't always feel this bad, and the more you allow yourself to go through your grief, the more quickly you'll get through it.

Facing It: This Relationship Is Over

At a certain point there is a quiet, dawning recognition that, yes, this relationship really is over. Yes, all these signs, indications, and subliminal fears are adding up to the reality that this relationship isn't going to be revived. Even though you would be willing to bargain your life or your consciousness away to save your relationship, it just won't work. There will be no mending, no renaissance of this relationship.

"My bargaining isn't going to work. I tried everything. I offered him the moon; I tried it all. And nothing worked. And now reality is setting in, and I'm getting used to the idea that it really is going to be over. It really is over."

This experience of facing reality often follows the period of mourning in which you are still connected to the hope for a miracle: "I'll do anything, just say it isn't so." At the same time, the very presence of your tears is an indication that on some deeper, almost primitive level, you have faced the fact that there will be no rescue, no return.

After this interlude of grief, after this cleansing by tears, there is often a time of dazzling clarity in which you say to yourself, "Now I can see it; it really is over."

"I don't know why, but after days in the pit of desperation, tears, wild promises, hope, it just came to me like a sign on a billboard: It's over. After that, although there was still a lot of recovering to do, I found myself mobilizing for whatever was ahead. My last hope had died. I had crossed some emotional line."

For most of us, there is a moment or a subtle emotional season in which the knowledge that we have tried to suppress rises irrevocably to the surface. After that moment of recognition, the healing process begins, for until we have faced the fact of the ending, we cannot begin our journey of healing.

It's All My Fault

Incorporating the reality that the relationship really is over involves trying to understand some reason for the ending, to devise some way of talking to ourselves about it. One way or another we have to explain to ourselves why this had to happen. Usually, the first explanation a person offers to himself is, "It's all my fault. I shouldn't have been so wrapped up with my work. She's right. I should have spent more time with the kids."

"It's true, I really was a slob. It's true; I never did do anything around the house. She's right; I never did share my feelings with her. I did keep everything to myself. It must have been like living with a statue. In fact, now that I think about it, I don't know how she's put up with me all those years."

"I was awful, chauvinistic, self-absorbed. I really did treat her like a second-rate citizen; I really did want the impossible from her. I really was an unconcerned lover; I really was an inconsiderate jerk. She's right. I took her for granted. I treated her like a wife; she wanted to be treated like a person. I'm terrible. I'm a terrible person. Now my relationship is over, and it's all my fault."

"It's all my fault. I did spend too much time with the children; I did make my kids my first priority. It's true; I ran around the house like a slob. I only got dressed up for church or when I went out to lunch with the girls. He's right; I gave the best of myself to everyone else and he always got the dregs."

"It's true; I did behave like a spoiled princess. I did go berserk with the credit cards. No wonder he hates me. No wonder he's leaving. And yes, I did keep harping on him about everything under the sun. No wonder he felt as if I didn't really care about him. I did expect him to solve everything. He's right. I did take him for granted. I know I've been passive; I know I never stood up for myself. I should have gotten angry. He would have respected me then."

At this point in the process, trying to devise an explanation for what has occurred, a million forgotten things come to mind, a lifetime's worth of all the crimes and failures we have committed come to the surface with startling swiftness and clarity. As long as a relationship continues, these things remain submerged and life goes on, but when a relationship is ending, we are forced to see it as a whole, as the totality of all our actions and choices within it. Suddenly, all our misdeeds and failures rise to the surface, and, in reaching for a reason why our relationship has ended, we look to ourselves and presume that, in fact, we might have had more control. "I know why this is happening," we finally conclude, "it's all the things I did—or didn't do. It's all my fault."

This is a very easy position to come to because none of us is perfect; it's true that within our relationships we have all acted badly, rudely, crudely, unkindly, selfishly. Here, at the end, looking for an explanation, we reach for the handiest one, an awareness of our own mistakes. "Of course," we say to ourselves, "I'm bad; no wonder it ended. It's all my fault."

At this point, we expand all our crimes to giant dimensions in order to try to explain to ourselves what has happened. We think of everything we did as having monumental significance. We believe what we did caused the relationship to end and so there's a tremendous amount of guilt. This is the point at which we contact all our limitations as persons.

When a relationship is working and is happy, joyful, and successful, nobody says, well it really is of ultimate importance that I don't roll the toothpaste up right, or it really is of ultimate importance that I went to sleep tonight without saying "I love you," or it really is of ultimate importance that sometimes I show up in the house with my hair curlers in, or that I flirted with my best friend's wife at the party—because those things are all part of the background. But when it stops working, all these things come into the emotional foreground. Suddenly they take on huge meaning, and we sit there beating ourselves up: "It's all my fault."

This willingness to take on blame is a kind of further desperate extension of the bargaining process. We are saying, "Is there any way, if I make a complete, total list of everything I've ever done wrong, that you'll take me back and we can start over again?"

This is a very dangerous phase of the process because it's very easy to get stuck at this point for the rest of our lives—to continue to describe the ending of the relationship as a personal failure and to ascribe the reason for its ending as having to do with specific inadequacies in ourselves.

Because this phase represents such a gigantic assault on self-esteem, it is a very important phase to get through, and one of the ways to get through it is to turn over and look at the other side of the coin. It's important to remember that whenever you are in a relationship, there are undoubtedly things you've done wrong and should feel guilty about. There are also things you've done that the other person didn't like but that don't necessarily represent personality disorders or flaws in your character. There are things in our natures which, while they may be aggravating to the person with whom we were in a relationship, are not necessarily bad traits in themselves. It's also important for the person going through this phase of ending to realize that feeling guilty is normal, but it is also very important to be efficient in identifying real guilt and then moving beyond it.

It's All Your Fault

Since our old mythologies of love would have us believe that love is perfect, exclusive, and forever, if your relationship has ended, it's obviously somebody's fault; and if it isn't my fault, it's got to be yours. As we noted, the first impulse for most of us is to take the blame on ourselves, to focus on our own inadequacies and failures and to decide that the "failure" of the relationship had to be our fault.

When this feeling becomes too uncomfortable, like a hair shirt you finally want to take off, the feeling that comes along next is "It's all your fault." It's time to spread the guilt around.

"It's all your fault, you selfish slime; you never did care about me. You could only think about yourself, your career, your friends, your health, your weight, your problems. It's all your fault; if you hadn't had that affair, we'd still be together."

"It's all your fault. If you'd gone to church, if you'd spent more time with the children, if you'd ever helped around the house, if you'd made more money, if you'd talked to me instead of retreating into yourself, if you hadn't been such a hopeless workaholic, if you hadn't been such a tyrant, if you hadn't had such a temper. If you didn't drink, we'd still be married; why, we'd still be in love."

"It's all your fault, you lousy, self-indulgent bitch. If you'd ever grown up, we might have made it. You didn't care about me."

"It's all your fault. You're way too uppity. You never should have gone back to school. It's all your fault. It was all those lunches with the girls, all those corporate meetings, your fancy new career. You changed."

"It's all your fault. You were so goddamn uptight about sex. No wonder I had those affairs. You made sex an ordeal. You always had a headache. It's over and it's all your fault."

At a certain point in the parting process, we're all inclined to say, "It's all your fault. It's over because of you. It all has to do with your personality—your anger, your nagging, your hysteria, your self-indulgence. You're the one who ran off and had the affair, after all, and if it weren't for you, this marriage would be just fine."

Allow yourself to go through the blaming. Realize that it's a natural stage to go through, that it's one of the ways in which you explain to yourself why your relationship ended. You must realize, of course, that your partner, too, will go through this stage. He or she is entitled to blame you for your real crimes, and he or she may also go through a stage of wildly inappropriate blaming in order to deal with all the hurt feelings and the incredible sense of loss. A warning, however. It's really easy to get stuck at this stage and feel victimized by your former partner. All too many people spend years—or even the rest of their lives—wallowing in self-pity.

In order to end a relationship and not feel fragmented, "crazy," and confused, we do need to understand why it ended, and in order to understand, we have to try on all the reasons (my fault, your fault, God's fault) that might apply. We need to go through the whole spectrum of explanations until, having covered all the ground, we can release the relationship and go on. So enjoy your heyday of blaming and self-pity, but then care enough about yourself to get on with the next step of the process.

Just Because You Asked for It Doesn't Mean You Want It

So, you've been fed up for years and finally you've had the courage to end your relationship: one of the surprises and turnarounds that often occurs in endings is that very often the person who initiated the ending goes through a loop of retroactive panic, terror, and confusion and finds himself suddenly saying, "Oh, my God, I've really done it, and now I'm not sure this is what I really want."

"When I told him a couple of weeks ago that I wanted to break up," said Lynn, "I was just testing him; now I wish I hadn't said some of the things I said, because then he started feeling that way, too. I had no idea he would take me seriously. I knew we were in trouble. There were so many signs that the relationship was ending, and I was so fed up with him that I thought I really wanted it to end. But I had no idea that he would take me up on my offer. I wanted him to change so we could go on. I guess I was really the one who didn't want to see that our relationship was ending."

"I haven't seen her for a couple of weeks now or even talked to her," said Jim. "I miss her, I guess. I know I'm the one who wanted to do this, but now I'm starting to wonder. Maybe I was a little too hasty. Maybe what I wanted isn't possible. I don't know. When I think back, we did have lots of really good times. I've been on a few dates—disasters, all of them. I've spent a couple of nights in the bars. It's a jungle out there. I'd forgotten about all that. I'm feeling very confused. Sometimes I think I made a really big mistake."

This feeling often comes along a couple of weeks after either the emotional or circumstantial reality of the ending has set in. The immediate feeling of exhilaration that accompanies having made the decision has started to fade, and now reality—the empty bed, the boring Saturday nights, the quiet house, the dinners alone, and the perfectly rolled-up toothpaste tube—has started to set in.

Even when we're sure we want to end a relationship—when we have clearly identified the reasons—there is often a backlash such as Lynn and Jim describe. That's because no relationship is totally bad. If it were without any redeeming qualities whatsoever, you wouldn't have been in it in the first place. Often, after you have made a decision to end it, a decision which is based on all your negative feelings, the positive feelings, which were there all along, come back, like the ghost of Hamlet's father, to haunt you.

Sometimes the person who initiates the ending has not really done all the emotional work that's necessary to really be comfortable with his or her own decision to end it. Many times, people who ask for the ending get cold feet and end up saying, "Please come back; I didn't mean what I said," or they go through severe emotional trauma because they've asked for something that, in fact, they're not emotionally prepared for. They think they're fed up. They think the last thing they ever want to do in the world is wake up and see the other person's lousy face again. But when the separation begins and they have the experience of waking up without that hateful face beside them, they are suddenly afraid. They're confronted with themselves, and it becomes clear that all the problems in the world really weren't caused by the other person. In fact, maybe the other person really wasn't so bad after all. One woman said at this point, "I don't know what was so bad about life with my husband that this is an improvement."

Does this feeling at this stage mean that the person who has ended the relationship really wants to get back together? Sometimes it does, but what it usually means is, "I'm scared. I've made a big decision here, and it's scary living out the consequences." Or, "I've made a big decision, and I'm finding out some things I didn't really want to know. I really thought all the problems were because of him, but now that he's gone, I see that the problems are still here. Maybe these are my problems."

If ending the relationship has been a way of obscuring your own problems and if you decide to make this ending the occasion for dealing with them, it may turn out that you will want to go back to the relationship. But usually, if you've actually come to the point of stating that you want the relationship to end and followed it through with action, despite whatever flaws and problems you may uncover in yourself, it's very likely that your relationship does need to end.

If you're still having second thoughts at this point, it's because you're scared, and you need to face the fear on its own terms and find some ways of dealing with it. If after dealing with your fears you find that your relationship still captivates you, then you need to reevaluate it. You may go back to it for a while and sometime later start the whole process of ending again. But generally, if you've arrived at this point, most likely you really have come to the place where you want to end your relationship; you're just suffering emotional backlash.

Going through this stage is more common for the person initiating the ending, because the initiator has to carry the emotional burden for the decision and has to believe that the right decision has been made for both people. It is at this moment of somewhat artificial certitude that positive feelings about the relationship do tend to come up as a kind of backlash. This is a very difficult time to get through because all the good parts of your relationship do deserve to be acknowledged: "Oh, yes, I see it isn't really black and white; there are still some positive feelings. I still have touching memories—we used to have so much fun. I can think back to when we first fell in love and that night we went canoeing on the river."

These are the kind of painful, touching memories that can come back and remind you—even though you thought you were so absolutely sure it was totally and completely over—that there were good things and good times in the relationship. Their emergence now can be terribly confusing, and so it is important to remember that it's highly unlikely that even the sweetest, most tender memory you can call to mind is reason enough to invalidate your decision.

Just Because You Didn't Ask for It Doesn't Mean You Don't Want It

Just as the instigator can get caught short by contacting positive feelings about the relationship after deciding to end it, so also does the "victim" have a surprising stage to go through. The person who is being informed that the relationship is over, the poor baby who is being left, often languishes longer in each of the early stages I've already described, especially the "I can't believe this is happening to me" stage. Although this person hasn't been going through all the thought processes at a conscious level—that, yes, the relationship is over—finally, he or she does get the message. Following this acknowledgment, there is a shift in which the person being left connects with the possibilities that exist beyond the end of the relationship. In other words, this person is almost glad it happened.

This is always very surprising.

I think the reason this happens is that the person who is being left gets thrust very profoundly into grieving right away: "Oh, I remember all the nice times. Oh, what about the children?" "Oh, but I love you. Oh, how can this be happening? I'll be lost without you. I'll die. I'll never love again." The "victim" is forced into deep grief and, as a consequence, into the cleansing that grieving provides and then is ready to begin again. These people find that on the other side of the grief there is always a new beginning. When the "victim" is finished with grieving, he or she is often amazed to have stumbled into it.

"I thought I would die," one woman said, "I mean really, literally die, when he told me he was leaving. I just couldn't conceptualize life without him—after twenty-four years of sleeping naked next to him.

But somehow I got through all those suicide days one day at a time. Then one day I realized, hey, I'm still alive, there actually are some good things about living and I might as well see what there is to do with myself.

"That was the turning point for me. Suddenly I stopped feeling like a victim and I had this wonderful sensation that someone had given me another chance, a chance to experience life in a way I had never expected—as a single woman, with my own consciousness, as the architect for all my choices. I had married 'till death do us part' and I'd never expected that I would again experience life on my own.

"I discovered that the life I wanted to lead on my own was very different from the life I'd been leading with him. His leaving was the beginning of my development as a person. In a way, I really thank him."

This, by the way, is often the theme of those who have "been left": surprising gratitude. Many people who have had their relationships ripped away from them later on feel that the opportunities and the development that followed included things that they never would have had the courage to pursue for themselves had they not been "abandoned." They often find themselves feeling oddly grateful to the person who "ended it," "broke their heart," or "left."

Sometimes this takes a good deal of time—years later when another, more appropriate relationship has been established ("I never would have met Paul if Bill hadn't left me")—or sometimes it happens very soon, when loose personal threads are gathered up again very quickly.

Phil recovered quickly. His wife came home one day and "out of the blue announced that for two years she'd been having an affair with one of our best friends and that she was moving in with him. I was in total shock. I didn't have time to consider anything. She told me, she packed her bags, and she was gone. It was as if fifteen years had been excised, surgically removed.

"I followed her dramatic example and ripped the house apart from stem to stern. I turned her sewing room into a study. I bought a new bed and masculine sheets, and I started doing all kinds of things I hadn't done for years—working out, going out, taking myself and my goals more seriously. There was an aggressive competent part of myself that I had 'mislaid' in the course of my marriage. When my marriage got peeled off like a skin, there was my self, just waiting to jump into action."

The amazing surprise is that after going through the stages of ending, you discover that there is life after the end. That in itself is a gift. What the quality and content of that life turn out to be is even more surprising. I have never yet talked to a person who has gone through the process of the emotional resolution of his or her relationship who says, "I wish I were still there; I wish this hadn't happened." In spite of the pain, the universal feeling is that the ending was appropriate and the gifts of the relationship were many. (Nor, by the way, do I find people saying they wish the relationship hadn't happened—even though now it has ended. All agree that something of value was given in the relationship and that still more things of value were collected when it ended.)

Very often I see the "victims" in relationships get through the process of emotional resolution about their endings more quickly than the people who initiated the endings. In my opinion, this is because these people are forced to do their emotional work. They don't have a choice about it. They are devastated and they have to find a way to survive. They have to find a way of interpreting both their relationship and its ending to themselves, and so they really push through the feelings that need to be gotten through in order to bring them to the point of emotional resolution.

I'm Not Myself Anymore

Somewhere in the midst of ending your relationship, you'll find that you're just "not yourself anymore."

Any relationship—even a bad one—represents a steadying influence in our lives. On every level it provides definition for us, for what we think, feel, and hope for, and both directly and indirectly it provides guidelines for how we behave.

For example, when we're in a relationship, there is generally one other person who knows where we are and what we're doing, who has some expectations about whether we're going to be drunk or sober, who knows whether we smoke or not, who knows when we go to work and when we're likely to come home, and who probably knows too what is likely to set us off at work and what we need as an antidote to a bad day at the office or a boring day at home with the kids.

In the subtlest of ways, then, a relationship defines our habits and behaviors. Not only does it set limits for us, but it also provides opportunities. It allows us, for example, to be sure of having a date for the movies; it provides us, generally, with someone to talk to over the dinner or breakfast table; it gives us the feeling that someone is curious or concerned or even angry about our whereabouts. A relationship provides a point of reference, someone to check in with, another consciousness in the universe that reacts to or reflects our own.

When a relationship ends, all of this structure—both that which is clearly identified and acknowledged ("We always went to the movies together on Friday nights") and that which occurs on a subtler level ("He's my rock," or, "She's the only one who really cares about me")—starts to crumble and is gradually dismantled. We find ourselves without rules, without the underpinnings of familiar habits and rituals, and without the benefits that they provide.

As a result, people find themselves functioning in what feels like a random universe and behaving in ways that seem uncharacteristic to them. They find themselves not doing a lot of things they did when they were in the relationship or doing one or a number of things they never expected to find themselves doing.

"I started smoking again. I hadn't smoked for five years, and then I started again."

"I started smoking. I'm forty-two years old and I've never smoked. Can you believe it? Starting to smoke at age forty-two?"

"I got arrested for drunk driving. I can't believe it. No, I can believe it. I've been drinking like there's no tomorrow. Drowning my sorrows."

"I've lost ten pounds. I just can't eat."

"I've gained ten pounds. The only thing I can do is eat. I wander around the house like a zombie. And eat."

"I quit my job. As long as she was around I could stand it. I felt like I was working for something. Now everything seems meaningless."

"I cut my hair. I don't know why. I just chopped it all off."

"I got five traffic tickets. My driver's license is on probation. I've driven for sixteen years and never gotten a ticket. My mind is always somewhere else. I'm a maniac on the road."

All these behavioral changes indicate that the ending of a relationship is exceedingly stressful. We react to this stress by adapting our behavior and adopting new coping behaviors, even if negative, as quickly as possible.

But transformations in behavior are not only an acknowledgment of stress, they are also the frontier of change, the invitation to change. In a sense, the ending of a relationship says to us: Look what's changed already; are you willing, do you have the courage and the daring to make some other changes too? This is your chance.

As a result, it is very often the case that tiny habit changes during this painful transition period are the first archings-up in what eventually become dramatic new personal trajectories.

Repossession of the Self

One of the other things people feel when their relationships have ended is an awareness of how much of themselves they have "given away" or disowned or invested in the other person or in the relationship itself.

What follows is often a time of relocating the self that was subjugated to the relationship itself or to the person to whom one was related. This discovery—this time of repossession of the self—is always an exciting one. "I took out my golf clubs for the first time in fourteen years," Sam said.

"It's been so long, I wasn't even sure I still knew how to use them. My wife always objected to my playing golf. She thought it was a mindless game and resented the money I spent on it. I don't even remember when exactly, but one day years ago I put my clubs away, and that was it."

"I'm wearing lipstick again," said Jessica, "and jewelry, and colors I haven't worn for years. I don't know what it was with Phil—whether it threatened him, or whether he genuinely liked a more organic look—but he always had a fit whenever I wore lipstick. I used to hide it in my car, like a sneaking adolescent, and put it on when I was going someplace where I wanted to feel pretty and dressed up, but if I came home with it on, he'd have a fit—the way women do when they find lipstick on their husbands' collars. It was ridiculous. I feel as if I've re-owned my glamorous self; I'm being the woman who really loves to dress up. That really is a part of me and I realize now how long I've been crippled, trying to look like somebody else."

Another form of repossession involves time. Lee said he couldn't believe all the time he had now that his relationship had ended. "The whole time I was with Irene I never felt as if my time was my own. Do this, do that, fix this, fix that. I never realized it, but now that I have all this time back, I feel as if there are a million things I want to do."

Sally, a woman who felt as if her home had been her husband's castle, initiated a project of repossessing it. "I decided," she said, "that I was going to remove or change everything in the house that was a reflection of him. I bought sheets with flowers and lace, the kind of thing he wouldn't be caught dead in."

Time and again, people surprised themselves with their changes.

"I joined a gym."

"I started running. It was a great way to get rid of tension and start feeling healthy."

"I've never been interested in ballet and now I'm taking a class."

"I've become a total hermit. My relationship was a giant distraction for me. I've been afraid of being alone, of getting to know who I am. Now, finally, I'm getting to know myself."

"I've become a social butterfly. I've always been shy. I used my husband to protect me. Now my protection is gone. I've had to go out on my own. I like it. I'm finding that I'm really quite a social being."

"I changed my wardrobe. She was always the clotheshorse. I figure, it's my turn now."

"I went back to school. He was the focus of my life and now that he's gone, I had to think of something else."

"I quit law school. I didn't want to be a lawyer anyway. That was her dream."

"I got a new job. I thought, what the hell, he ditched me, I might as well try something new—so I did."

"I started having fun. The whole time I was married I was so goddamn serious; I was always paying the bills, fulfilling my responsibilities. It didn't pay off. Now I realize there's more to life than work. I've started to play."

"I quit smoking. I realized that smoking was a death trip, that for years I hadn't felt like being alive. Now I feel wonderful. I feel as if I've been reborn."

"I quit drinking. We were in a self-destruct conspiracy. After she left, I realized I wanted to be conscious—all the time."

The repossession of the self marks a turning point in the process of parting. At this point, the wound is beginning to heal. You have survived the dark night of all the negative feelings. Now, because of what transpired in your relationship, you can encounter essential characteristics, talents, inclinations, and perspectives that may even have been obscured since childhood. And the more you regain your lost self, the easier it is to let go of the relationship which has ended.

Something Snapped

People sometimes say to me, "Well, he's gone," or "She's moved out, but how do I know that it's really over? It still doesn't feel like it's over."

Even after all the stages we have already described—even after you've moved out, even when the ink is drying on the divorce documents, even when you've turned in your engagement ring to the diamond broker—there are little loose ends and linkages of attachment that remain, little voices that come up and whisper, "Are you sure you've done the right thing? Are you sure it's really over? No turning back? No taking a breather and then starting over?"

Somewhere along the way in the evolution of this parting, there is an event that makes it very clear at the deepest emotional level that the relationship is not ever going to work, even though there are those residual twinges. I call this phenomenon the point at which "something snapped."

Sometimes it's that parted lovers, afraid of their decision, get back together for one more lunch, or one more dinner, or one more roll in the hay, and during that encounter something happens that reminds them, in a dazzlingly vivid way, that it's absolutely right that the relationship has ended—that last little piece of resistance to the ending has snapped.

"We'd been split up for three months, and then one night I just had this weird impulse to sleep with him again. As usual, our sex was mediocre, but what really put me over the edge was that in the middle of the night he rolled over in bed and hit me in the eyeball with his elbow. I felt like I'd be blinded for life. For me, that's when something snapped."

"For me it was when we went out to dinner after we'd been separated for six months. Bob had four drinks before dinner and wine with his dinner. He was so loaded he could hardly walk out of the restaurant. Then he said, 'How would you like to go somewhere for a drink?' That's when I realized he really had a serious drinking problem. I saw that nothing—not even losing me—had motivated him to do anything about it."

One woman said, "When I came into the kitchen and saw that he hadn't washed the dishes—again—something snapped." Another woman said, "I don't know why, but for one more time he said he wouldn't go out and look for a job, and that was it. It was over." One man said, "Something snapped when she ran the charge account up over the limit that last time. I realized that was it. The final thread of connection had been broken."

A businessman said that for him something snapped the night he had some difficult clients to entertain. "I called my wife and said, 'Honey, please come out and help me,' and she said, 'I can't; I'm too tired.' I could understand that she was tired, but somehow this particular time was one too many for me. I realized that's who she was. She wasn't going to change."

All these people are describing a moment of insight, a keen awareness that brings them to a turning point. It is suddenly crystal clear that the relationship is over. This may occur during the process of parting, it may be the event that precipitates the parting, or it may not happen until long after the break-up has been completed.

In the process of weighing and sorting the long ambivalence that ending a relationship inevitably is, there is always a moment that marks the point of total disillusionment. This moment can be as trivial as coming home and finding that once again your wife hasn't made dinner or as devastating as the discovery that your husband truly is a child molester. Either way, it marks the moment that I call "Something Snapped," the moment when you realize there is no turning back; the essential connection is broken.

The Little Door to My Heart Is Closed

After something has snapped, after you've left the apartment or gotten the divorce, after you've dated someone else or a dozen someone elses, after you've tried out your crumply wings of new independence, after you've remade your wardrobe, your hair style, your exercise habits, after you've started drinking more or less, after you've quit smoking or started smoking—after all this, you wake up one day and notice that "the little door to your heart is closed."

What this means is that at the deepest levels of your consciousness the emotional charge of the relationship has been neutralized. Now instead of thinking of the person you once loved with longing or regret, with anger or resentment, disappointment or sorrow, you think of that person simply as someone you've known, as one of the people who has been a participant on your journey. In the same way that we make dear friendships in school, at summer camp, in the service, through therapy groups, church, Alcoholics Anonymous, bridge or exercise clubs—and then end those friendships because our circumstances change—so it occurs with old spouses, lovers, and sweethearts. We eventually get to the point where we are no longer actively emotionally involved with them.

"It's been four years," one woman said, "and I've been a basket case most of the time, but last week his mother came to visit and we all went out to dinner. I looked across the table at him and said to myself, 'The feeling is gone. I don't even have to dislike him anymore.'" That was her way of saying that the door to her heart was closed. He no longer had the capacity to engage with her emotionally.

Arriving at this place where the little door to your heart is closed can take a very long time or for some people whose relationship has been in a state of disarray or dissolution for quite a while not very long at all.

"For years, every time I saw him," Phyllis said of her husband of thirty years, "I still felt pangs of sorrow and resentment. But then one day he turned up unexpectedly at my grandson's birthday party and . . . nothing happened. I was amazed. He'd lost his power over me. He was just an attractive, middle-aged man I remembered knowing a long time ago. There was no longer a pull toward me. We're not going to be friends, but we don't need to be strangers."

"It took ten years for the door to my heart to close on my first wife," Stuart said. "The relationship ended. I went on, got married again, had children, but there was this very painful place in me about her. We were so young when we got married, and our divorce was so traumatic, that I realized I'd lived through my whole second marriage still thinking of her. It wasn't until my second marriage ended that I realized I still had unfinished business with my first wife. I contacted her, and fortunately she was amenable to talking with me. We went over all our resentments; in a sense, we finally got to know one another, and finally I resolved that relationship. Now I feel free of her; for the first time I feel capable of making a new relationship."

What Stuart is referring to is the point of emotional resolution about a relationship. As he indicates, it is an absolutely critical point to arrive at. We can't make new loves if we are still carrying around blame, resentment, and self-pitying mythologies about a relationship that has already ended. As long as we are still emotionally engaged in the old relationship, we are unavailable for any satisfying relationship that may follow. I can't say this often enough because even people who insist that they want a new relationship are unable to form one if they haven't let go of their feelings about an old love. This was never more apparent to me than in the case of a seventy-three-year-old woman, terminally ill but still raging about a marriage that "ended" thirty years before. Unable to forgive, forget, or resolve, she had spent her whole life without love, endlessly cataloguing the failures of her former husband.

Saying the door to your heart is closed does not mean that you have no appreciation for what was given to you. It also does not mean that you can't be objective about the wounds or disappointments that you suffered. The key word is objectivity. When the little door to your heart is closed, a lot of doors to your mind are opened. When we are in love, we are prejudiced in favor of the person whom we love; when love has ended, in order for us to truly be ourselves again and in order to love again, we must establish a clear, unprejudiced picture of the person to whom we were formerly related.

Nostalgia, the recollection of fond memories, is different from emotional resolution. In fact, feelings of nostalgia and appreciation can be experienced much more easily after the little door to your heart is closed. Your memories are like postcards from another time, which you can take out, look at, cherish, and enjoy.

Just as you can still have appreciative feelings when the little door to your heart has closed, you can also still have negative feelings about your former spouse. Especially if you have children, you may, and very likely will, encounter circumstances that can generate anger, irritation, and frustration. But the difference will be that these feelings are generated by specific contemporary circumstances—not by unfinished emotional business. Just as our best friends, a store clerk, and the gas station attendant are all capable of making us irritated and even angry in the present moment, so do our former spouses and sweethearts have that capacity if in the present we have a difficult exchange with them.

One of the reasons children of divorced couples become the objects of ongoing displays of emotion between former spouses is precisely because one or more stages in the emotional resolution of their relationship have not been completed, and the children become the vehicle for this unfinished emotional business. Parents who have resolved their emotional business with former spouses—even if the opposing spouse refuses to do his or her own emotional homework—are clear in their relationships with both their children and their former spouses. It's only when feelings haven't been identified and dealt with that problems continue to arise.

Whether or not there are children involved, closing the door to your heart marks an important passage in the ending of a relationship. Rather than being the negation of a relationship, arrival at the place where the door to your heart has closed marks the celebration of the fact that you have finally completed the process of emotional resolution. You have moved away from the relationship on every level, your emotional state is clear, and you're ready for whatever comes next in your life.

6

The Unconscious Process of Parting

INVARIABLY WHEN A RELATIONSHIP is ending, our dream life communicates to us about where we are in the process of parting. On an unconscious level, you chart the process of parting, from the first incredible shock—"I can't believe this is happening to me"—to the point of emotional resolution when, finally, the little door to your heart is closed.

Not only is the process of parting itself charted in the unconscious, but often when a relationship is in trouble, there are dreams that foretell the parting that is to come.

One woman reported to me that for years she had a dream that she was moving from the house in which she was living with her husband. She was very happy in her house and these dreams were so upsetting to her that she classified them as nightmares.

It wasn't until several years later when her husband revealed that for a long time he had been having an affair that she learned the real meaning of her dreams. They were her unconscious radar picking up on his infidelity, her premonition that, in time, she would have to leave the house she loved. This is exactly what happened when subsequently they were divorced.

When the ending is actually starting to occur, when on a conscious level the person is saying, "My God, I can't believe this is happening to me," the unconscious reflects on the disaster that is occurring, appropriately enough, by producing images of this disaster. People going through this stage of parting frequently report having dreams in which the symbols are earthquakes, typhoons, tidal waves, bombings, flash floods, or fires.

One man came into my office and reported that "out of the blue" he'd had a very disturbing dream in which his house was totally destroyed by an earthquake. His marriage had been going through a difficult phase for some time, but when he reported his dream, I felt that the "disaster" would be close at hand. It was the following day, in fact, that I received the phone call in which he told me his wife had announced she was leaving. On an unconscious level, he had already received the terrible news and had reported it to himself in the form of his dream.

One woman said that when she realized her relationship was ending, she had a dream in which she saw the whole world as a planet that was a barren wasteland. A new ice age had arrived, almost all vegetation had died, humanity had disappeared, and as her dream ended, she was huddled down in a field of tall, dry grass waiting for the arctic air, which, no doubt, would freeze her to death.

Her dream was an image of the feeling many of us have that life isn't worth living when our relationships have ended, that the whole universe has changed, that reality isn't what it once was, that life itself won't go on.

Another woman recounted a dream in which she and her husband were driving along a coastal road and, on a perfectly beautiful sunny day, an immense tidal wave rose up, causing them and their car to be carried off to sea and become totally submerged. Somehow she managed to swim to shore as the tidal wave subsided, but her husband and the car were lost forever in the depths of the sea.

Interestingly, it was she who survived the tidal wave of her divorce. Her husband, who had always had a serious drinking problem, reacted to the divorce by drinking even more heavily and eventually got into an accident that caused him serious injury.

People who feel guilty about their role in the demise of their relationship often report dreams in which they see their guilt. One man saw himself locked in a room and being taunted by all the women with whom he had been unfaithful to his wife. A woman who felt her passivity was her contribution to the ending of her relationship saw herself in a dream as a sickly, speechless child curled up on a chair under the kitchen table. As the dream progressed, the child was awakened by a visiting tyrant who ruthlessly, cruelly punished her and then left. This was the image of her passivity in her relationship and of its consequences. She pictured her husband as "the visiting tyrant" who punished her and then left.

During the stage of anger and blame, people report dreams in which they experience themselves doing violence to their former spouses, sweethearts, and lovers in what is often a frightening way. One woman reported seeing her former sweetheart driving up a circuitous mountain road, wishing and then watching as his car flew off the edge of the cliff, crashed, and burned. Another woman saw her husband being executed by a firing squad with herself as a hooded, incognito member of the firing squad. Still another woman reported having a dream in which she used her culinary expertise to bake a poison cake for the man who was leaving her. "I remember having a lot of trouble in the dream figuring out just how I was going to get the poison into only his part of the cake," she said.

Dreams of murder and violence are characteristic of the emotional stage when feelings of deep disappointment, anger, rage, and betrayal are being processed. One terrified man confessed that he dreamed of strangling his wife. Another dreamed that he arrived at a grave where a stone bearing his wife's initials had newly been set in. "I knew I had something to do with her death," he said, "but somehow in the dream I didn't feel bad about it; I felt relieved."

Another man saw his wife being buried and suffocated in a mountain of credit cards. In his dream, he punished her that way; in reality, he felt that she had punished him.

Although these dreams of violence are often reported with a mixture of embarrassment and terror, they mark important turning points in the healing process. For it is when the deep anger at our partners is acknowledged at the unconscious level that a resolution to the anger is beginning to occur.

Although these dreams generally make people feel very uncomfortable—the uncovering of any repressed feeling is generally accompanied by a significant degree of discomfort—the acknowledgment of the dreams and in particular the reporting of the dreams are very important. This is because when we report our dreams out loud, we are bringing up to a conscious level the feelings we have repressed and which, as long as they are repressed, will impede our further progress. When we bring them up to the level of consciousness, we are allowing ourselves to make the information they contain a part of our working reality.

Thus, bringing to a conscious level feelings we fear are unacceptable is a very important step in the process of emotional resolution. If you can, write down your dreams or talk about them with someone, because it is exactly at the point at which we can start living consciously with our formerly repressed feelings that we have completed one stage of healing and are ready to move on to the next one.

What I'm saying here is don't be afraid of your awful dreams and nightmares. They are telling you that you are moving appropriately through the process of parting and that just as you have completed the scary stage, so you will go on to stages of deeper resolution, and even to the stage of wonderful new possibilities.

For example, at the "Something Snapped" stage, people often report dreams that symbolize breaking and shattering, a final severance of some kind. For one woman this was the image of the ropes of her backyard swing suddenly snapping and causing her to fall to the ground. For someone else it was the image of a door to his wife's dressing room slamming shut and magically locking her inside: "I knew it would never open again." Another man had a dream in which he saw a young boy sitting beside a pile of twigs, taking them one by one into his hands and breaking them in two. In his dream, he was breaking all ties to his former life.

At this stage also, another person reported repeatedly having the dream of being in a classroom and having the blackboard wiped clean. "That was it," he said. "I'd sit in the classroom, and someone— a little boy, I think—would come in and wash the blackboard clean. And then the dream would end." His dream was the image that the slate of his relationship had been wiped clean. There was nothing more to be said or done about it.

Another dream that is typical of this stage is a dream in which the former partner is seen at a great distance. "At the beginning of the dream, I saw us walking through a meadow together," Jan said, "and as the dream progressed, two paths diverged in the meadow, he went off to the left and I went off to the right, and after a little while, he had walked so far that all I could see of him was a little speck in the distance."

Another image of emotional distancing—the acceptance that the final connection has been broken—includes seeing the face of the former beloved in a crowd. One man had a dream in which he saw his former wife's face in a crowd, first as a blur, which when it came into focus he momentarily recognized as his wife, until the image blurred again. "She faded in and out," he said. "The interesting thing was that when she faded out, I didn't care. I guess that's the way she is for me now—just an unfocused face in the crowd."

When an emotional resolution has occurred at the very deepest levels and we can both perceive and conceptualize the person we have loved with objectivity, the imagery of our dreams goes through a dramatic transformation. For one thing, images referring to the former partner diminish and disappear (to make only occasional, random future reappearances), and the imagery of the dream is much more focused on the emergence of the self. This indicates that life is no longer focused on the lost relationship, but on the personal renaissance. At this stage, people often have dreams that include the most classical images of new beginnings, frequently the appearance of a new baby (the self beginning to be born again), the tiny seedling of a plant, or a dream that is only a landscape or an ambiance. "I saw a beautiful meadow," one woman said. "The feeling was one of clarity and possibility. I felt as if I'd moved into a totally new and different dimension, and when I woke up I felt all sparkly and fresh, as if something essential about me or my world had changed."

When the process of healing is complete, and the survivor of the lost love—the person who, for a long time, believed that he or she would never love again—is capable of getting ready to love again, the faithful unconscious provides another metaphor. One woman dreamt she had gone to "the court ball." "I was all dressed up in my finery without an escort, and then this huge gray cat walked into the room and wrapped himself around me like a lover.

"I embraced him and said, 'You seem so human, did we know each other in another lifetime?' For just a minute he turned into a beautiful, blond-haired man and whispered, 'Yes, I knew you once. At Christmas. You were a goddess. We danced.' Then he was gone. He had turned back into a cat.

Coming Apart

"I realized that this was somehow the image of the man I would love in the future. I wasn't yet able to see him as a man—that's why he appeared as a cat—but his loving kindness was irresistible. In the end, I did allow myself to see him as a man."

One man spoke of dreaming that unexpectedly he had come upon a single red rose blooming in his garden.

Another woman saw herself imprisoned in a cage and it was only when a man approached her cage and put his hand through the bars that they suddenly fell away and she walked out to embrace him.

All these dreams are the wonderful accompaniment to our emotional process, the way in which, in a sense, we hold our own hearts in our hands and become our own mirrors while we are going through the anguishing process of parting. Freud called dreams "the royal road to the unconscious." I would expand on that by saying that making the information of the unconscious available at a conscious level is the royal road to emotional resolution.

Although the remarkable, beautiful, and magical imagery of dreams and the wealth of information they provide cannot always be interpreted by ourselves for ourselves, it is of the utmost importance to assign significant value to the unconscious process that is occurring, to take it seriously, to treat it as a gift.

Perhaps these examples will help you identify the messages in your own dreams or inspire you to uncover their particular meanings with the help of your own therapist.

Sympathetic Phenomena

When our relationships are going through their various stages of dissolution, and while we are accompanying their dissolutions with the appropriate set of feelings, there is another unusual process that occurs.

I refer to it here as the occurrence of sympathetic phenomena. What I mean is that when we are ending our relationships, it seems that there are signs and symbols in the world around us that corroborate our experience. In a sense, it feels as if the universe itself is reflecting our experience of estrangement, pain, and loss.

Because our extreme emotional vulnerability during the process of ending makes us particularly receptive and extremely focused on ourselves, we begin to experience what is occurring in the world around us as being directed toward us or having specific meaning for us. For the grieving person it is as if, in a sense, the universe weeps with him. Whether or not that is true in some ultimate sense, it is certainly true that people going through the endings of their relationships report that what they see, hear, and learn from the people around them seem to intricately corroborate their own emotional experience.

One woman described it this way: "All the songs on the radio are about me. They're all about lovers leaving their lovers, they're all about wondering how to survive, they're all about the end of a love. It used to be that I only heard love songs: you're my darling; everything's going to be perfect; we're going to walk off into the sunset together—all that. But now—now all the songs are about endings."

"Everybody's breaking up—it's an epidemic," another man said. "I'm just part of the latest fad." He listed off the names of a couple of friends and acquaintances whose relationships were also ending. It could be that at any time in his life an equal number of friends and acquaintances were ending their relationships, but only now did it seem to matter, only now did it seem like an "epidemic." The news about his friends' dissolving relationships seemed to corroborate his own experience.

There are still more specific signs and symbols that people interpret as statements from the universe about what is happening to them. For example, one woman said, "Whenever I end a relationship my rose bushes die. When my first marriage ended, it was my very first rose bush that died. Ironically enough, it was called 'First Love.' My second husband was an avid gardener, and he bought me a very special rose bush, which he planted in the garden. As long as we were together, it bloomed in profusion, but sometime after he left, while all the other roses continued to flourish, 'his' rose started to languish. One day, six months after he'd left, I noticed that while every single rose bush around it was alive and well, his rose had dwindled down to a single gray little twig, and finally it died."

"Everybody looks like her," said another broken-hearted lover. "I swear to God. I walk down the street and every woman seems to walk the way she did. Dozens of women have her hairdo. I race to catch up with them, hoping I'll get a glimpse of her, but then they turn their heads and once again I realize that I've been following someone else. My secretary sounds like her. Sometimes even the time lady on the phone begins to sound like her. She's everywhere."

For some people the observation and corroboration of loss is not so consciously observed, yet these signs are received and recorded on an unconscious level. One woman, when asked if she had had any clues about the ending of her relationship, said that the day before her husband announced that he was leaving, she lost a ring he had given her when they first started dating. Another woman lost a pair of earrings that had been her husband's first gift to her.

Often the external symbol for the emotional loss is another form of loss—lost keys, lost gifts, lost memorabilia, and especially lost jewelry, because jewelry is so universally a gift that is given in the early, positive, romantic stages of love. This is not a coincidence, for when we shed a love we allow ourselves, and even unconsciously direct ourselves, to shed the symbols of that love.

While the unconscious and the material of dreams refer to the internalization of our emotional process about ending our relationships, what I call "sympathetic phenomena" refers to the externalization of our emotional process. In times of great emotional stress, it is natural to project our own experience into the outside world. We externalize our experience as a way of diluting its painful intensity. We lighten our own seemingly unbearable emotional burden by seeing what is happening as occurring, at least in part, outside of us.

One of the healing functions of all these observations and externalizations—of seeing the universe as expressing our plight, in particular—is that through these interpretations we come to feel less isolated in our experience.

If splitting up is "a fad," if the "roses die" when our hearts are broken, if "everyone looks like her," we feel that in some ultimate cosmological sense the universe is commiserating with us. This is terribly important because, as we indicated earlier, one of the most painful feelings precipitated by a parting is the feeling of being alone, especially in confronting our ultimate, existential loneliness.

While it's important not to carry these perceptions to a narcissistic or delusional extreme, there is a great deal of comfort that can be derived from feeling—and experiencing—that in some sense when we are sorrowing, the whole world weeps with us.

7

Binding the Wounds: How to Get Through the Ending

I HAVE TALKED AT LENGTH about the emotional process of parting and traced the various emotional events that accompany the conclusion of a relationship. It is my firm opinion that whenever we attend to our emotional tasks, the practical solutions follow. When our hearts and spirits are whole, then our survival instincts will be also. In chapter 9 there is a series of exercises that is specifically designed to take you through the emotional process of parting, binding your broken heart, and opening the way to the future.

But while you are going through this emotional process, your real life has to continue—you have to go to work, deal with your children, pay the electric bill, get the clothes to the cleaners, and keep groceries in the house. In a broader sense, you have to make the transition from being a person in a relationship to being single. In order to survive this time of transition, you need to develop a few specific survival techniques. This chapter is a little first aid kit, a set of bandages and medicines with which to cover your wounds until they have time to heal.

At precisely the moment when you think you have nothing going for you, when you think the one thing that held your life together—your relationship—is gone, you need to sit down and take account of what you do have to work with. You need to identify the resources in your life and draw up a list of what will serve as your support system. It's usually very simple—a catalog of habits, rituals, friendships, values, and ideas you can count on to take you through a heartbreaking time.

"I guess what I have to face," said Polly, "is just how I am going to get through the next few days without thinking of Tim every minute. I want to go home and call him right now, but I know I'll be sorry if I do. I know he'll just tell me again that it's over and I just can't stand to hear that one more time.

"I have my job, and I love it. I'm going to really dress up, and that'll make me feel good. There are a lot of people there who like me, and it'll feel good to go there every morning.

"I also have my church. I haven't been going there lately. In fact, I stopped going while Tim and I were together. He thought it was silly. But there are a lot of people there who know me, and I think it'll feel good to be there with them again.

"I ordered some new magazines. When I come home from work, if I have something easy to read, I don't feel as sorry for myself being alone.

"The one other thing I really want to do is take an exercise class. I've always wanted to do that, but I've never quite had the time. So I'm going to check around and see if I can find a class that fits in with my schedule."

Habits

Perhaps the most basic part of your emotional first aid kit is having habits you can rely on, things like that first cup of coffee, Friday night at the bar with the boys, breakfast in bed, a manicure, hot baths, new magazines, fresh orange juice, an after dinner walk. If some of your habits are essentially unhealthy (like smoking or drinking), this probably isn't the time to give them up, but try to avoid indulging in them to terrible excess. Identify those things in your daily repertoire that are really good for you and rely on them.

Old Friends

Another very important resource in making the transition out of a relationship is to hold on to what is familiar in the human dimension of your life. There's a big gap in your emotional life right now, and it's time to get some of your needs met by your friends. In order to maintain a sense of emotional continuity, it's essential to continue any relationships that are still appropriate and that still have meaning for you. "I don't know how I could have taken the breakup of my marriage without my next door neighbors," said Jack. "I think I ate dinner there every day for weeks."

Of course, one of the fears is that all your friendships are based on the unit of your relationship. The truth is, however, that each of us has friends who are particular to us as individuals. We don't only have friends as a couple. At this time, it will be very important to identify those relationships that are specific to you personally and make a special effort to make contact with those friends, to use them for emotional support, for sounding boards, for companionship, to meet some of your needs for involvement, participation, appreciation, and communion that were being met by your spouse or sweetheart.

Many women find that during this time they turn to a special woman friend who knew them during their relationship, and they see to it that this friendship is nourished. Men tend to turn to a sports buddy or business colleague because they know that these relationships will continue through the transition. This is a time in which, for reasons of continuity, you should rely on old friends.

New Friends

As I've already indicated, the end of your relationship marks the completion of a particular and important stage of development in your life. You have become a new person as a result of what has happened to you, and now you are ready—both in terms of romance and friendship—to make some new relationships. To that end, be open to people whose interests and values are a reflection of your new or rescued identity. New friends support emerging new identities, so take a chance—take a stranger to lunch. Enhance your chances for new connections.

Do Something Different

In a crisis, a basic therapeutic maneuver is to do something different. We need a balance between relying on what is so familiar and incorporating some things that are new. The way to get into the future is to take a risk—take up a new hobby, learn a new language, get the degree you've always been afraid to get, find a new sport, take the trip you were never able to take before.

All of these experiences have two positive effects. First, they give you an enhanced sense of yourself. They also provide you with opportunities to make new friends—friends whose interests reflect your own new directions.

Psychotherapy

If, after you have read this book, done the exercises, and counseled with yourself about the meanings of your relationship, you find that you are still unable to bring yourself to a point of emotional resolution, it would be wise for you to consider psychotherapy.

Because a psychotherapist, whether a psychiatrist, psychologist, or marriage and family counselor, is trained to see what you might prefer to avoid, they can often assist you in arriving at the deeper insights you need to feel resolved about your relationship. Since this is an extremely vulnerable time for you, however, you need to choose your therapist with care—and trust your feelings in the choosing. When we are bruised, we tend to feel that the very act of seeking help should help us. It is unfortunately true, however, that not all therapists are beneficial to their clients nor is any particular therapist necessarily right for you.

If you come away from your initial session or sessions feeling encouraged or enlightened, you're probably in good hands. If you don't, however, try another—or several other—therapists. Finding the right therapist is a little like buying a hat. Just because you try it on doesn't mean it's right for you.

Time

The statement that time heals all wounds is such a cliché that even the mention of time as a healer or as a critical dimension of the resolution process may seem either irrelevant or insulting. Nevertheless, it is patently true that time is a miracle healer. When we are going through a difficult experience, however, we tend to want to rush through it and we often lose patience—the one virtue that could most assist us. We want an instant resolution. We want deliverance now. We want to get through the feelings without allowing them to go through us. But whenever we try to shorten our emotional processing of pain, anger, and sadness, we inevitably lengthen it. This is a very hard thing for people to understand. I have seen dozens of people in pain not because their relationships had ended, but because they prolonged their pain by trying to avoid it.

When it comes to the matter of time and its role in the healing process, there are two things you need to remember: (1) Don't rush the process. Be sure to go through all the emotional stages of parting. Don't cheat—or you won't arrive at a deeply integrated resolution. (2) Realize that time must pass. Time will make what you have learned become an integrated and important part of you; in time, the pain will be gone and you will be a new person. Give yourself time.

Be Kind to Yourself

When we suffer some kind of trauma or assault, we often tend to exacerbate it by making further demands on ourselves or by having totally unrealistic expectations about what we can manage.

For example, if you're afraid of being alone in the house after your husband has left, give yourself permission to get a roommate or to move in with somebody else. There aren't any extra points for being brave—you've already been through a very tough time; now give yourself a break.

If you're a woman, perhaps you'd like to change your image: get some new clothes, get that snazzy short haircut. Buy yourself a nice present, some special perfume, sachets for your drawers, some new jogging clothes. Ask your mother to baby-sit so you can go out for a day. If the problem is time, get up half an hour earlier so you can spend some time with yourself.

If you're a man, try buying yourself a new sport coat, a new set of golf clubs, or a bevy of dramatic ties. Schedule a weekly manicure. Subscribe to the Playboy channel or a computer magazine. Go hiking. Go sailing. Play tennis. Go on a mini-vacation. Stay in touch with your children. Write them a letter; call them up on the phone. Take yourself and a friend out to a brand new restaurant.

When it comes to your children, don't try to be the perfect parent. A very important part of what your children need to understand about life is that it includes change, pain, and times of emotional trauma. You won't be able to come through in every single way they'd like. Explain this to them; allow them to enlarge their view of reality.

Beg mercy from friends if you are not able to meet your obligations to them as fully as you'd like. "I'm sorry, Jane, but I just can't keep our lunch date; I need to be alone." If you took on a lot of responsibilities when you were in your relationship and you can't fulfill them now, allow yourself to bow out gracefully.

If you thought your husband was going to support you in your old age and you find that you now have to go to work, don't expect that your house will be as immaculate as when you didn't have a full-time job. Don't expect to have all the free time for your friends that you had before you worked.

If, as a result of paying alimony and child support, you find yourself with a lot less money to spend, you need to realize that perhaps you are no longer in a position to be as generous or carefree with money as you once were. Try to see your present situation as an opportunity to use your resourcefulness and creativity. Develop other parts of your personality or see your belt-tightening as a challenge to create a new financial base.

In other words, don't be tough on yourself. Do whatever you need to pamper yourself. Give yourself permission to be in transition. Remember that you are going through a highly charged experience for which you have no precedent. It's very important that you be compassionate with yourself. You don't have to know all the answers; you don't have to be a hero in this situation. Respect your fears; remember that you are bruised now and you won't be functioning with the same degree of reliability that you normally do.

This transition time isn't just a test of your coping mechanisms; it is also an opportunity to come into contact with some of your long-suppressed and most precious attributes as a person. If you are willing to go through the difficult stage of applying these bandages very gently to your wounds, you may come to the end of this time to discover that without your even quite intending it, you have created a whole new identity for yourself.

8

The Postscript Relationship: An Antidote to Love

O NE OF THE DEEPLY FRIGHTENING things about ending any relationship is the fear that we will never love again, that the romance that has just ended will be the last love of our lives. For most of us that fear is so immense that it needs to be assuaged almost immediately as a part of our emotional healing.

It is because this fear is so pervasive that one of the most common phenomena that occurs after the ending of the relationship is what I call the "Postscript Relationship." The Postscript Relationship is a mini-rerun of the relationship that has just ended. It is a microcosm in which you can see quickly and vividly the things in the original relationship that caused its end.

Postscript Relationships have a number of specific characteristics: they are usually very brief in duration—a week to only a few months; they are relationships with a person who in some significant, and sometimes almost mind-bogglingly similar, ways resembles the person from whom you have just parted; and they create feelings that distinctly, specifically, and uncomfortably replicate feelings you felt in the recently ended relationship.

Because of these similarities of feelings and experience, the Postscript Relationship has a very compressed quality. It is a mirror in which we can evaluate the defunct relationship as its lessons are finally and forcefully driven home.

Postscript Relationships tend to be teaching relationships and not real romances. Their chief function is to transmit the lessons of the recently ended relationship; when this has been accomplished, they are generally ended with remarkable efficiency—and a surprising lack of emotional trauma. In fact, it is often only the repetitive aspects of the Postscript Relationship that draw you into it in the first place: people pick new partners who have the same jobs, the same habits or vices, or are the same body types as their previous mates.

In a surprising number of instances, I have observed my clients getting involved with a person who even has the same name as the person they have just discarded.

"Can you believe it? Jim. My least favorite name. I've just recycled one and another one turns up."

"That's right. It was David—and David."

"I couldn't believe it. Her name was Linda too."

"Susan. That's not quite Sue, but it's pretty damn close."

This is not, of course, specifically intentional, as the remarks above indicate, but it is significant because the name itself calls forth many meanings and feelings from the earlier relationship and, in itself, provides an opportunity for many evaluations of the earlier relationship.

In other instances, the similarities may run deeper than the repetition of the name. One woman who had just ended her eighteen-year marriage to a policeman who had green eyes and black hair found herself in a relationship with a retired policeman who also had green eyes and black hair.

In the Postscript Relationship, she experienced a rerun of all the conflicts she had felt in her marriage—a battle of wills which she had never been able to resolve and that had ultimately been the reason for her divorce.

"It was as if I needed to see it all one more time," she said. "I'd been through so much in the ending of my marriage that I couldn't see the issues anymore. But going through it one more time brought all the lessons home to me. Suddenly everything was crystal clear; the second relationship helped me confirm my decision about ending the first one."

A man who had recently ended his marriage to a successful attorney found himself briefly in a relationship with a woman stockbroker. "I couldn't believe it. I'd just ended a relationship with an aggressive woman, and lo and behold, I put myself in the same situation. There I was, feeling powerless again. There I was, hoping she would find some time for me. There I was, wondering whether she'd ever cook dinner for me, wondering if I would ever get a turn. It was all so painful and familiar. The familiarity was confusing at first—it felt like coming home—and then it was suddenly awful and immensely clarifying. 'Oh, my God, this is what I just left,' I said to myself. 'I can't do this again!' The night I figured that out—it was when I had taken her out to dinner for the fifteenth time in a row—I ended the relationship without a tear."

Other repeats run the gamut from "My husband always had to have control of the money and now I find myself going out with this guy who keeps track of every single penny" to "My wife was a secret alcoholic and I just found out this girl is half-smashed before we even leave for a date."

One of my clients found herself in a relationship with a man who drank too much, was violent with her, came from Montana, and had what she called "a Cro-Magnon consciousness." Six months before, she had divorced her husband, who had grown up in Montana and who, during frequent binges of drinking to excess, had been physically violent to her.

"At first I thought, 'This must be the way men are,' but then I realized it was me. I was doing the picking. I was choosing these violent men. I guess I just had to do it one more time so I could see what was really going on. Doing it again really helped. It helped remove the last shadow of a doubt about whether or not I was right to divorce my husband."

As her remarks indicate, the Postscript Relationship says, in effect, "In case you can't really believe what happened to you, we're going to run it by you one more time."

Although no relationship is ever completely perfect, and flaws and disappointments are to be expected, what is surprising in the Postscript Relationship is that we unconsciously direct ourselves toward an involvement that includes precisely the qualities and experiences that were finally unacceptable in the previous relationship. It is almost like viewing the body in the funeral parlor, as if you are saying, I want one last look before I really say good-bye.

Because it has so much to teach, it is important to evaluate the Postscript Relationship, to ask yourself how you feel about it, and to allow your experience to teach you what you still need to know about the earlier relationship.

Unlike the woman who momentarily assumed that her Postscript Relationship was simply an indication of "the way men are," we need to see these relationships as an opportunity for the final crystallizing clarification about the relationship that has just ended. Postscript Relationships provide an opportunity for deeper emotional resolution and prepare the way for new and more appropriate relationships.

9

Finding Resolution: A Personal Workbook

THERE ARE A NUMBER OF STAGES you will have to go through in order to feel resolved about the ending of your relationship. There's no getting around it. You will have to feel your way through all the stages in order to be emotionally finished with your relationship and ready to go on with whatever comes next in your life.

For example, you will have to go through the whole gamut of feelings outlined in chapter 5. You will have to go through the denial, through the explosion of tears, rage, and blame, through the bargaining, through the self-flagellation, through the moment of realization that the final thread of connection has snapped, and then finally, you will have to close the door on the relationship.

There are two other things you will have to go through in order to feel complete about the ending of your relationship. One is a change in attitude about the meaning of ending itself, a change of mind that says a relationship is allowed to end, to be gotten over. The second is the acceptance that the ending process isn't going to be easy. It isn't going to be accomplished, like dumping a bag of garbage or pulling a tooth. Rather, you'll find that it's a jagged process that takes you longer than you want it to.

Ideally, it would be wonderful if you could go through the resolution of your feelings with your partner, if you could just sit down and talk with him or her about all the things that went wrong and why it's right that you end this relationship. Since this is generally impossible, I have devised a series of exercises for parting in which you can go through your own process of emotional resolution. These are exercises for you to do by yourself, and they are specifically designed to help you move through the emotional process of ending your relationship and to facilitate your emotional resolution.

They are designed in such a way as to focus you so that any part of the emotional process that hasn't been fully resolved can now be completed. In other words, if you have any unfinished emotional business, these exercises are like a net that will catch them up and give you an opportunity to go through them. Without this structured approach, you could easily get detained or even stranded at a point in the process of parting. In fact, it's very easy to get paralyzed for a long, long time. I have had many people come to me for help in resolving relationships that ended five, ten, or a dozen years ago. It's clear you can get stuck at almost any point along the way. For example, one man in his sixties came to resolve feelings about a marriage that had ended when he was twenty-seven! These exercises will push you through those feelings so that, for example, if you're stuck at the point of blaming yourself or the other person, you can move beyond that point.

In the workshops where I have done these exercises, I found that whether or not people thought they had resolved their relationships, whether they were clear that they were still in pain and confusion, or whether they believed they would never feel resolved about their relationships, they all came away feeling they had moved into a state of deeper emotional resolution. Everyone said they learned something about the relationship they had never known before and, as a result, were now able to let it go. Over and over the comment was, "Now I understand; now I feel ready to move on."

There are five exercises, each of which has several parts. They are not to be done on the day you get the news your relationship is over. Rather, they are a process to do after you have gone through your own set of feelings about the ending. In order to receive the maximum benefit from them, you should do the following things: First, take these exercises seriously. This isn't like doing a crossword puzzle or reading an article in a magazine. Get yourself a notebook for this purpose so that when you are finished with the exercises, you will have them all together in a specific place where you can refer to them. They are the record of your emotional healing.

Second, allow yourself plenty of time. Provide at least half an hour, or preferably an hour, for each exercise. Settle yourself in a quiet place and choose a time when you won't be interrupted. Don't do this in the middle of the afternoon when the kids will barge in from school, or in a rush before you leave for work.

Do the first exercise and allow it to sit for a while. You may feel eager to go on to the next exercise, but since the exercises are dealing with deep emotional material, time will be required for assimilation and integration. You may want to go on to the next exercise right away, or you may want to wait several days or even a week before you begin the next one.

Read through each exercise and the examples before you begin to write. Don't hurry as you do each exercise. This isn't a speed contest. What you want is to allow enough information and enough feelings to come out so that you will be uncovering the material that can actually provide resolution. Don't be concerned with perfect sentences or perfect paragraphs or with what you wish had been true. Express your true feelings—in most cases these will be the words and feelings that jump instantly to mind after you have read the question.

In other words, express whatever comes up, whether or not you feel it "makes sense," is embarrassing, or is something you wouldn't want anyone to know.

Exercise 1: Telling the Love Story

When you get to the point of ending a relationship, you usually want to forget that you were ever in love in order to minimize the pain you feel now. But that's cheating. In order to really get over a relationship, you have to re-feel your way all the way through it, starting from the beginning, when you fell in love. After all, if you hadn't fallen in love, it wouldn't be so awful to fall out of love; if something hadn't captivated you originally, it wouldn't be so hard to let go now.

So rather than avoiding the memory, which is the source of pain—and also of healing—begin by telling the story of your relationship.

A. Tell the story of how you fell in love. Include where you met, what attracted you, what there was about the other person that seemed to resonate with some deep wish or need of yours.

B. Tell a little bit about the early stages of your relationship—your first date, your first brief interlude together. Remember—and write down—the feelings you had at that time, and also include your expectations. Because of your good feelings, you developed some expectations for this relationship. They were either conscious or unconscious; some of them were appropriate and were subsequently fulfilled, and some of them were way off the mark. Don't go into what finally occurred. Go back to the original time and your first feelings and write down the expectations you had. What did you expect would eventually occur in this relationship?

C. Write about what I call the "Clue of Failure." At the beginning of every relationship, there is a little clue that registers (and is subsequently disregarded). It tunes you into the fact that something will go wrong eventually, that the relationship isn't going to last forever. It may be a very odd thing.

One woman said, "I don't know why, but when I saw his tiny little bottom teeth, I knew it wouldn't work out." It turned out later that the man, who was physically immense, was, in fact, a very passive person, and it was his refusal to deal with his passivity that, in the end, caused their relationship to collapse. Somehow, at an unconscious level, her focusing on his little teeth was her awareness that he was not big, strong, and powerful, but a very passive person.

Another woman said that the man she was breaking up with swore too much the first night they went out. He was very generous, attentive, and appreciative of her, but as their relationship evolved she realized that his crude speech was an early indication of what later turned out to be an uncontrollable temper.

The point here is that there is always a clue—something that registers on a subliminal level and is subsequently disregarded, which is an indicator of what eventually occurs.

Here is an example of Exercise 1:

I met him at a party given by mutual friends when I was traveling. I was very uncomfortable at the party and he was the only person I could really talk to. I guess that's what really attracted me to him. That, and his looks. He was tall, dark, and handsome, but the thing I really liked about him was the comfortable, intelligent conversation we had.

How did I feel about him after the initial encounter? Really sad. I felt like, oh, here's the kind of man I could really like a lot, the kind of man I could really talk to and be comfortable with. Just my type, but he lives 3,000 miles away. Longing. I guess that's what I felt. I hoped—but I couldn't imagine—that we would ever meet again.

Expectations? Well, we did meet again, on another occasion, arranged by our mutual friends. Somehow it felt like we really belonged together, and we decided we'd work out the distance. I expected that because we had "recognized" each other so quickly that we'd have a perfect love. All the barriers would be taken away. I also expected, because he moved across the country to live with me, that everything else would be perfect, too. I suppose I expected that he would always sacrifice for me, just as he had by moving, that we would grow old together, that our life would consist of thousands of wonderful conversations like the one we had that first night.

What was the clue of failure? Well, I did notice, even that first night, in what I felt was a really wonderful conversation, that he talked an awful lot about himself. I was enjoying listening to him; I liked what he was talking about, but afterward there was this little edge of feeling that he was a lot more interested in himself than he was in me. I discounted it, though, of course.

Now write your love story.

Exercise 2: Telling the Real Story

We all have a particular mythology we tell ourselves about every romance we get into. That's the "love story"—the story in which the original meeting is fated and magical, in which we "fall in love," and in which—we assume—we will go on "living happily ever after."

The love story embodies the illusion, romance, and hope of any romantic relationship, whether or not that relationship eventually manages to be translated into a long-term love relationship.

As we have seen, by looking more closely at what is actually going on in our relationships, we discover that there is another reality that is simultaneously occurring—the developmental process. Exercise 2 is designed to help you discover the developmental process that was operating in your relationship.

A. First, write about what was going on in your life when your relationship began. What were you and your partner each trying to accomplish when you met? Were you starting a business, wanting to have children, trying to get a graduate degree?

B. Talk also about where you were in terms of relationship status. Were you waiting for a new relationship? Had you recently come out of a relationship? Were you in the middle of another love affair?

C. What was your developmental task? What was your partner's developmental task? Were you trying to get the good mothering you never had? Incorporate your sexuality? Gain a sense of your power, beauty, or intelligence? Understand your father's unavailability, your mother's possessiveness?

D. What was your gift to him or her? What did he or she give you? An example: He helped me believe that I was a lovable person and I rescued him from his mother's clutches.

E. How did the Clue of Failure ultimately manifest itself? For example, the person who had one too many drinks on the first date turned out to be an alcoholic. The person who didn't want to get together until next week turned out to be unavailable for a relationship. The person who was overly generous turned out to be a spendthrift.

F. If the story of your relationship was written up as a novel or made into a movie, what would it be called? Some examples include: *Great Expectations, Two Ships That Should Have Passed in the Night, The Year of Living Dangerously, More Is Less,* or *Two Many Gin and Tonics.*

G. What was the real reason your relationship ended? This reason has to do with the completion of your developmental task. What task did you complete? What task did your partner complete? Some examples: "I outgrew my need for a mommy." "I finally got in touch with my power." "We finished raising the children." "It was all sex; that wasn't enough."

Here is an example of Exercise 2:

When I met Hank, I was a wallflower type. I think I must have been very pretty as an adolescent, but no one had ever told me, and so I'd grown up, gotten married, and lived for years as a Plain Jane, responsible housewife. That's who I still was after my first divorce, and that's who I was when I met Hank.

Somehow he saw me differently. It was as if he reached back to my forgotten adolescence. He allowed me to blossom. He treated me as if I was beautiful, and so I became a beautiful woman with him. The ugly duckling turned into a swan. I finally came into possession of my beauty and my sexiness.

As for my gift to him, what I think I gave him was his masculine power. He'd been floundering with his business for ages. He needed a beautiful woman at his side, a mascot, someone to make all the risks and hassles of doing business worthwhile. I became that focus, and his business started taking off.

I believed in him and encouraged him—no one else had done that—and then he started believing in himself. He started taking the chances he needed to take in order to succeed.

I suppose a good title for this relationship would be Beauty and the Business Man. *I got the gift of my beauty, and he got the sense of himself as a competent man in the world.*

The Clue of Failure in our relationship was the anger I felt in him the very first night we met. Along with really enjoying me, focusing on me, and telling me how beautiful I was, he expressed a lot of anger about other people and things. I found this difficult. As time went on, I also began to wonder if this wasn't one of the reasons he hadn't succeeded in business. He couldn't manage his anger. For me, that was the thing that ultimately broke our relationship. I couldn't handle being the sponge that had to absorb his anger. Even his adoration of me wasn't enough to compensate. His anger was so powerful—it seemed to come out of nowhere on a moment's notice—that in the end I couldn't stand it. I was always walking on tiptoe for fear that something would set him off.

I can't speak for him, of course, but I'm sure there was a clue for him also. He often said he felt from the very beginning that I wasn't "available" to him. I think that's true. I'd just come out of a long-term marriage and I wasn't ready to get into another serious relationship. I wanted to play. I wanted to be a carefree adolescent. I think he finally got sick of waiting around and trying to convince me that I could get into another serious relationship. I think he hated my tenuousness, my exploratory, what-else-is-out-there state of mind.

Why did the relationship really end? As grown-ups, we weren't a very good match. His business really bored me. I couldn't imagine a lifetime of hearing about it or of absorbing his anger about every little thing that went wrong with it. I wasn't captivated enough by him as a person. I was captivated by his response to me, by his attention to me, but I wasn't really captivated by him.

The other reason is that once I had gotten a sense of my sexiness and my prettiness, I wanted to try it out. I wanted to test it out in the world. He wanted me just to hang around, to be pretty and his mascot, but since I'd solved the wallflower problem, I was ready to move on. There were a lot of other things I wanted to do with my life.

He wanted a conventional relationship where the man works and the wife is beautiful. I wanted to grow, to expand to my fullest dimension. In the end, we weren't really a very good match.

Now write the real story of your relationship.

Exercise 3: Facing the Ending

It's all well and good to do the retrospective analysis on your relationship so you can start to understand it. While all these ex-post-facto insights are terrifically beneficial and it's great to put the love of your life in a box, label it, and consign it to your personal emotional archives, there is also the problem of your pain. What about the ouch, the incredible pain of ending? What about getting through all the anguish?

Along with learning, that is, understanding what transpired, there is also the emotional process of going through the feelings that are occurring as the relationship grinds inexorably to its anguishing conclusion. Now it's time to deal with those feelings. This exercise, which has six separate parts, is designed to move you through these different feelings to the point of resolution. Once again, remember that each exercise takes time. It may be days or even weeks before you are able to move from one part to the next. Remember that you are not just writing, but also feeling your way through.

A. Something Snapped

Go back to the point at which "something snapped" for you. Where was that turning point? What was the word, incident, encounter, or betrayal that was the breaking point for you?

"It was after I'd supported her for six months in her search for herself, without any balance of support for me, that something snapped. She asked me to do the laundry one morning, and I just couldn't handle it. Something snapped. I knew we'd never make it."

"It was when he came home drunk for the four-hundredth time."

"It was when he turned down that job offer."

"It was when she forgot to call me after her meeting, for the five-thousandth time."

Now write about the moment when "something snapped" for you.

B. The Sour Grapes Inventory

Now make a Sour Grapes Inventory; that is, make a list of all the reasons why it wouldn't have worked out anyway.

Sometimes when a relationship has ended, we indulge in all sorts of "if only I had" or "if only she or he had." But when a relationship ends, one thing is clear: all the resources that both of you had at the time to develop or sustain your relationship weren't enough to sustain it. Instead of indulging in a lot of self-destructive nostalgia, it's much healthier to sit down and tell yourself why it wouldn't have worked out anyway. This will help you to affirm what has occurred and perhaps even tell you why your relationship should have ended long ago.

Here are some examples:

"He's way too dependent on me. He can't figure out what to do with his life; forty years old and he still doesn't know what he wants to be when he grows up."

"He isn't tall enough. In the end, I really couldn't handle having a lifelong relationship with a midget. It was great to have an intimate sexual relationship with him, but in the long run, I can't have a relationship with someone I'm embarrassed to be seen with on the street."

"She's too young. The truth is that in time those fifteen years would make a difference. Beauty is great for passing romance, but in the long run we wouldn't work out in real life."

"He doesn't talk enough. I really can't handle his silence. I can't stand his lack of communication. I need someone who will really talk to me."

"He was too arrogant. I tried to roll with it, but in the end he was incorrigible. It got too tiresome. I can't handle being with someone who always has to be right. I need life to have an easier flow."

"She was too hysterical. She was wonderful and exciting and I loved to look at her, but her hysteria was deadly. It took so much juice out of me. I really can't stand it, living every day wondering if I'm going to come home to my loving wife or a raving bitch. I need more evenness than that."

"She wanted to talk too much. She wanted more intimacy than I could handle. A relationship isn't my form of entertainment. I really prefer my work. I always felt like I wasn't giving her enough, and I couldn't stand feeling that bad about myself."

Now think about why your relationship wouldn't have worked in the long run and write your own Sour Grapes Inventory.

C. The Poison Pen Letter

Whether you made the decision to end your relationship or had it made for you, you are probably feeling an incredible amount of anger.

We don't like to have our footings ripped from under us; we don't like our own particular realities to change. When this happens to us, we want to blame our partner for the awful out-of-control feelings we are having. Sometimes these feelings are so intense we feel we'd like to get even.

Angry and, in particular, violent feelings are very scary. We usually want to inhibit them or disown them. They certainly don't fall into the category of any feelings our mothers ever told us were acceptable. But in order to heal from the devastating wound that ending a relationship is, it is important that we also experience these vile, rotten, intense, and unacceptable emotions. In order to get beyond them, it's important to go through them, to give them full rein, to allow them expression—but in some way that is not, in fact, destructive, so that we can get beyond them.

A very good vehicle for this is what I call the "Poison Pen Letter." In this exercise, you will write a letter to your partner in which you express the full intensity of your rage, your most vile intentions about him or her, and your most self-indulgent wishes for his or her demise.

The purpose of the Poison Pen Letter is to allow you to give expression in fantasy to these intense feelings without harming yourself or anyone else.

Here are some examples:

Dear X,

> *For starters, I hate your guts. You are a self-righteous, greedy egotist. You sit around telling other people to take risks while you, yourself, are a coward in the emotional vulnerability arena. You are a controlling, manipulative, self-centered egotist. You are selfish, self-centered, self-indulgent, and not a good enough person in your own right to recognize any of these things about yourself.*

> *You may think I am broken-hearted because you've changed your mind, baby, but I'm not. I'm lucky you busted me out of my own masochistic streak. I hope you self-indulge yourself out of every relationship you ever have a chance at. You missed a beauty, sweetheart. I hope you rot in hell.*

Dear X,

> *You are a double-crossing, two-timing, arrogant jerk. I can't believe you lied to me like that. "Integrity," you always said. What you know about integrity could fit on the head of the pin. You lied and then you lied about lying. You drove me crazy with your lies and then made me feel as if it were all my fault.*

> *I hate your guts for that. I hope you meet somebody and trust somebody who lies to you the way you lied to me. Then you'll know how great it feels. I hope it drives you crazy too.*

Now write your Poison Pen Letter.

D. Feelings of Failure

Next, write about your feelings of failure. There are two kinds of feelings of failure that can get mixed up. One bunch is the self-destructive, self-loathing feelings of failure: "I'm not good, it's all my fault, I've blown it forever." The other is a set of feelings that do have to do with your own real and very specific failures in the relationship.

First, indulge yourself in all your self-flagellation. Get it off your chest.

> *"I am no good."*
> *"I should have tried harder."*
> *"It is all my fault: he was perfect; I'm just not any good."*

Then move on to a real accounting of your failures in the relationship. In any relationship longer than a week, we can all do things that are inappropriate, inconsiderate, mean, hateful, selfish, or just plain bad. When you come to the end of a relationship, it is important for your own healing (so you don't walk around for the rest of your life carrying a tattered knapsack of guilt) to acknowledge that you, too, weren't perfect. You did do some pretty lousy things. You weren't a god or a goddess in the relationship; you were a mere human being. You hurt and betrayed and ignored the person you loved. It is very important now to truly face your real failures. Don't get defensive about them. It really could take forever to get over your relationship if you can't acknowledge your crimes, so list them now. Write them down—as fully and as feelingly as you can.

> *"I was too financially self-indulgent; I did go crazy with the credit cards and put us in a bind."*
>
> *"I didn't take enough chances communicating with him. I let my fear overtake me. It must have been lonely, living with me."*
>
> *"I was a pushy, aggressive jerk. I pushed her around instead of listening to her. No wonder she felt unsupported."*
>
> *"I was a terrible slob. It must have been hard to live with my mess."*
>
> *"I was a fantastic perfectionist. It must have driven him crazy, living with someone who had to pick up every speck of dust."*

"I did drink too much. I am an alcoholic; I wouldn't face that. I feel terrible about the night I drove the car into the tree."

Now list your own authentic failures in the relationship. Don't ignore real faults, but also don't exaggerate.

E. The Letter of Confession

The cliché that confession is good for the soul is a cliché precisely because of the truth it contains. In order to have a clear conscience—and thus a clear consciousness—when we end a relationship, it is of critical importance not only that we acknowledge our real failures to ourselves, but also that we confess them to the person we have wounded.

So now, write a letter of apology for all your crimes to your old sweetheart, partner, husband, or wife. In this letter, be absolutely ruthlessly honest in identifying what went wrong, and be absolutely crystal clear in your apology. This is a letter for your benefit. Its purpose is to cleanse your consciousness and it need never be shown to your partner.

Dear X,

I am writing to tell you how sorry I am for having an affair while I was still involved with you, and then for lying to you about it. I know this made you feel crazy, and I am very sorry for messing with your perceptions in this way.

I know how terribly painful it is to have your sweetheart end your relationship by getting involved with somebody else. I am so sorry that I chose this indirect, underhanded way of telling you that I was no longer happy with you and that I wanted to end our relationship.

I hope you will forgive me for the pain I caused you and I hope that in time you will be free from it.

Dear X,

Please forgive me for being such an inconsiderate jerk, for always refusing to wash the dishes, for calling you a dumb broad. I really am very sorry that instead of supporting you and encouraging you, I chose to criticize and put you down. I didn't feel very good about myself and I tried to make myself feel better by picking on you. I was wrong. Please forgive me.

Dear X,

I'm sorry I was so unaware of who I really am. I'm sorry about all the double messages I gave you, for telling you that I really wanted to be with you, when, in fact, I only wanted a very minimal relationship. I didn't know myself what I really wanted—but that's no excuse. I made you suffer for my confusion, and I'm sorry. Please forgive me.

After you've written your letter, ask yourself if it really expresses specifically and completely what you did wrong. Have you asked the other person to forgive you? Have you "eaten crow"? Have you expressed all the things about which, in your heart of hearts, you really do feel bad? Be sure you do, or you won't get the relief you need from writing this letter. You have to express it all. What is important is that at the deepest levels of your consciousness you have acknowledged your failures and you have admitted them to the person you have offended. When you have done this, you will be clear to move on.

Now write your Letter of Confession.

F. Letter of Forgiveness

There's one more part to this exercise, and that is writing yourself a letter of forgiveness. So you were a rotten, self-indulgent, controlling, lying, cheating, manipulative, double-crossing, slimy creep. You, too, are just a human being, and you need to forgive yourself for being just that.

Dear Me,

I know that I was an angry jerk over and over again in my relationship with X. I'm scared of so many things that sometimes the only way I can protect myself is by being angry. I'm sorry I did that to her; God knows, I've learned a lot from it. I'm going to stay in therapy until I learn how to temper my anger, but I forgive myself for being who I was at the time. I did the best I could.

Dear Me,

I know that I sent an awful lot of mixed messages about whether or not I was really available to be in a relationship. I was a tease. I'm sorry about that and I forgive myself for that. I really wasn't sure at the time whether or not I wanted to be in a relationship at all, and more specifically, whether I wanted to be involved with him. That was confusing I know, and I'm sorry. But that was the best I could do at the time.

Dear Me,

I know that I was a silent, uncommunicative partner. I know I punished and blamed instead of asking and telling. I'm sorry about that. It was my failures in this relationship that taught me a lot about who I am as a person. Losing her was a hard way to learn my lesson, and X doesn't get the benefits, but I forgive myself for being where I was and who I was then.

Dear Me,

I know I was an out-of-control lush when I was involved with X. He complained about it and he was right. I had a lot of pain I was trying to handle very inefficiently by drinking. Now that I've quit drinking I know that, and I forgive myself for being who I was then.

Now write your Letter of Forgiveness.

Exercise 4: Taking the Gifts

At the end of any relationship, there is a legacy that needs to be acknowledged. It consists of all the gifts that were given and received, the lessons that were learned, the changes that were accomplished. When we're going through all the pain and heartache and anguish of ending, we're not inclined to stop and take note of the benefits that we've received, but oddly enough it is at precisely this point that it is important to give thanks.

You may feel that you gave everything and didn't get a thing in return, but when you really stop and think about it, you'll realize that of course you did get something for yourself—at the very least a companion for the duration of the relationship. It's really important for you to stop and take note. You have received much, for every relationship enlarges and enriches us, changes us somehow in the interior and essential fabric of ourselves. Unless we take note of that fact, we will carry a grudge—instead of an open heart—into the future.

So now write a thank you letter to your former partner or sweetheart. What are the gifts you take away from this relationship; what are the gifts that you specifically received?

Dear X,

Thanks for everything. I was so unhappy before I met you. I really had no hope. The time I spent with you gave me the feeling that maybe life could be okay, even happy. Even though you're gone now, I still carry that feeling with me. That was a wonderful gift.

You changed my outlook and I will always thank you for that from the bottom of my heart.

Dear X,

I guess what you gave me was a sense of my power. I never really thought that I'd amount to anything. I was a slow starter, a late bloomer. I never got any encouragement from anyone but you. Somehow, because you believed in me—and because I experienced a certain amount of success while I was related to you—I started believing in myself. I miss you terribly, but your gift remains. Now I know that I can cut it in the world.

Dear X,

Thanks for our two beautiful children. If it hadn't been for you—for us—they wouldn't exist. You and I have gone our separate ways, but those two special children we created will always be a part of us and a statement about the life we had together. Thanks for giving me some offspring to enjoy. Without them, I'm afraid I'd be lonely in my old age. Watching them grow up has brought me an unbelievable amount of pleasure.

Dear X,

Thanks for helping me through school. Not only did you give me a lot of encouragement, but you also gave me all that financial support. I would have given up if it hadn't been for you. I needed to get my degree. You stood beside me. Thank you.

Dear X,

Thanks for giving me my body and my health. Before you came along, I took my health for granted. Your conscientious example had an incredible impact on me. Now I exercise and take my vitamins. I love to go biking and hiking and skiing. Thanks so much for giving me this part of me. I will be grateful always.

Now write your Letter of Appreciation.

Exercise 5: Redefining Reality

Now that it's over and you've gone through all the tearful, sorrowful, raging, self-blaming, blaming, and forgiving feelings that comprise the emotional progression of ending a relationship, you've come a long way toward your emotional healing.

But you still have the future to consider. How are you going to manage your feelings in the future? Specifically, how will you deal with the fact that the person to whom you were related is not going to drop off the edge of the earth? You may very well run into her in the supermarket or see him at your favorite restaurant with, God forbid, *somebody else*. How are you going to handle that?

Our tendency is to talk about our former spouses and sweethearts in the negative: "That creep," "That bitch," or in historical terms, "My ex." But when we refer to our former partners in this negative way, we not only stay connected to them, but we also stay invested in bitter feelings that inhibit growth. When we refer to our former partners with the historical "My ex," we keep one foot cemented in our history. In effect, we treat our past as more important than our present—or our future. In order to move ahead and meet and inhabit our futures, we need to create a new definition of the person from whom we have separated, and with whom, in a sense, we have created a new relationship.

One of the things we're afraid of when a relationship ends is that we will totally lose the person we have loved, that he or she will utterly vanish from our world. The truth is, however, that even though the relationship is over, the person we loved can still inhabit our emotional world. This becomes possible when we redefine the relationship by assigning a new identity to him or her. What I mean by this is that psychologically we can form a new connection with the persons we have loved by creating a different role for them in our own minds. This has nothing to do with whether we ever see them again. It simply means that we think of them differently. Instead of thinking of them as lovers, sweethearts, or spouses, we see them as having a different kind of connection to us. Assigning this new identity to your former partner is what I call the "Redefinition Ritual."

A. The Redefinition Ritual

Create a new identity for your partner. What was and is an essential aspect of your connection to him or her, which will always be there, even though you are not sharing an intimate romantic relationship?

Some options include father, mother, uncle, big or little sister, big or little brother, colleague, boss, employee, business associate, friend, enemy, intellectual compatriot, health consultant, financial advisor.

One woman told me: "After the dust settled, I started thinking of him as my little brother. He was always so sweet and adoring. I'd always wanted a little brother and he fits the role. Defining him this way allows me to keep the affectionate feelings I really do have for him."

Here are some other examples:

"An enemy. I'm not bitter, but he really is a bad person. I really made a mistake, getting involved with him."

"Daughter. I was her protector and I showed her the way. She grew up and left me. As a daughter, she's a sweetheart; as a wife, she was hopelessly immature."

"A consultant. I know I can still call him when I need help with my taxes. That was a very important role he played for me. He helped me get my financial life squared away. I know I can always turn to him for that and that feels good."

"Pin-up girl. She was my Marilyn Monroe calendar. Now that I've gotten over her, I see she still is. I keep her photo in my office as a beautiful woman to inspire me. No matter who comes next, she'll still be there, like the pin-up girl a man has as a secret from his wife."

Now create a new definition for your former partner.

B. Defining the New Frontier

Now that you've read this book and gone through these exercises, you should understand that underlying every relationship there is the accomplishment of one or more developmental tasks.

What is your developmental task right now, at this moment? What is your psychological growing edge? What are the most important qualities you need from the person with whom you form your next relationship?

For example, a woman who had just earned a law degree said, "I've had it with study and self-discipline. Now that I've got my career in the bag, I want to explore my feminine side. I'd like to keep a journal, read more novels, take more time for my emotional life, dress up more, and pamper myself. Any man who will fit in my life will have to be a professional who can accept that I work and appreciate the feeling side of life."

A man who had just seen his youngest child through college said, "Now it's my time for me—to stop working so hard. I need to start enjoying myself, to take better care of my body.

Any woman who gets involved with me will have to share my athletic pursuits."

A woman who had been married for twenty-three years wrote, "I have to become independent, to grow up, I guess, and stand on my own two feet." No matter how unclear your developmental tasks may seem to you, it is nevertheless true that as surely as you complete a relationship, you will be embarking on a new developmental task. If you have difficulty identifying it, think what your closest friends have remarked and observed about you lately, pay attention to the issues that cross and recross your own mind, or if you feel really in the dark about where you're heading, consult a psychotherapist.

Now, in order to create a new reality for yourself, write about your next developmental task and what you will need from the next person in life.

If you have been steadfast in working your way though all these exercises, you should now feel that the pain of your ended relationship has been excised. You have understood the projects and meanings of your relationship, you have forgiven yourself and your partner, you have received a plentitude of gifts. By allowing yourself to know that every relationship not only invites, but also propels you into the future, you can face what before felt like the frighteningly uncharted territory of your future with a newfound sense of direction, confidence, optimism, and excitement.

10

Is There Love after Love?

A RELATIONSHIP—THE UNION of two people at work and play and in shared circumstances with one another—serves many functions in our lives. It provides emotional communion, circumstantial companionship, an environment for childrearing, an economic back-up, and, as we have discovered, it is also the medium for the accomplishment of many developmental tasks. Thus it is that, on an unconscious level, when we establish a relationship, we are not just "falling in love," we are choosing the person and kind of relationship that will help us accomplish our task of the moment.

The value of taking stock when a relationship ends is that it teaches you a lot about who you are and what your developmental task has been. If you pause to evaluate your old relationship, you can see what your next developmental task is likely to be, and you can create your next relationship out of a much more highly developed self-consciousness. You can choose someone who is a more appropriate partner for you, both in terms of your emotional preferences in your life and values, and your growing edge as a person.

What people always want to know when their relationships are ending is, "Does this mean that I will never fall in love again? Does this just go on forever, the doing of developmental tasks?" Well, obviously, if you continue to have relationships, there is going to be one that lasts "till death do you part," even if it's number fifty-four!

But there is also a point we all come to in life in which we have pretty much accomplished our essential developmental tasks. Eventually, we all get to the place where—except for fine-tunings and refinements—we have learned basically who we are. We've sorted out our preferences from the vast number of possibilities we all have as human beings, and we know what we want to spend our lives doing. Generally, there is a fail-safe point at which we have constructed our identities and where we are ready to live the rest of our lives out of the amalgam of those identities. This is the point at which we can make a relationship that lasts a lifetime.

Along with being prepared for love in a developmental sense, however, there are some things we need to know about loving itself. Just as we haven't been taught about endings, so it is even more sadly true that we haven't been taught about what goes on inside the house of love. We are untutored in love; we don't know how to conduct, maintain, or sustain our loving relationships. We train ourselves to become machinists or marine biologists, but when it comes to our loving relationships, we are virtually uneducated.

What forms the basis of a relationship that lasts is positive, loving feelings and the awareness that you each have a whole complex of attributes that are of value to the other and give pleasure to the other. "He always knows what to say to bring me out of my funk." "She's just so beautiful; whenever I see her face, I'm overcome with joy."

These positive loving feelings are easily sustained when there is commonality. By commonality I mean there are a great many ideas, preferences, values, and perceptions that are held in common, as well as appropriately matched levels of physical and emotional energy. Commonality means that you can both, on any day of the year, say, "Yes, we'd love to go sailing today because the weather is gorgeous," because you both love to sail. Or, "Yes, we'd love to go to the art museum" because it never fails that when you look at great art, your spirits are moved, and you feel happy with each other.

"We have an incredible sex life. We can't resist each other. No matter where things go wrong, we always find our way back together in bed."

"We both love to walk. We both have this passion for nature. It never fails to make us happy. We never have conflict about what to do if we have a spare minute or two."

"We love to travel. We've traveled hundreds of thousands of miles together."

"Faith. It is our faith in God that holds us together."

"Our children. These three beautiful kids we created and our endless fascination and delight with them."

"Tragedy. We went through a lot with the death of our child. It bound us up in a very deep way."

"Dancing. We both love to dance. Whenever we have a free evening, we dance."

"Struggle. We were both alcoholics. We met in AA. The recognition that each of us had conquered a terrible addiction gives us respect for each other. I don't think I could feel that for someone who hadn't had to struggle through such a nightmare."

"Flowers. I know it sounds crazy, but we both have this inordinate appreciation of flowers. Even when we are at each other's throats, if we go for a ride and see something in bloom, there's an incredible softening toward one another."

"Intellectual rapport. I never get tired of talking to her. Her mind is a feast for me. I love the way she thinks. I never stop learning from her."

Commonality means that if you're a fanatic athlete, you don't want to make a relationship with a horn-rimmed intellectual who's afraid to catch a breath of fresh air. If your one remaining wish in life is to have children, don't choose a man who's had a vasectomy. If you're a woman and you've finally defined, after years of struggling toward it, that your career is really the most important thing to you, don't choose a man who wants an old-fashioned wife. If you're a man who's learned how to cry and express your emotions, don't pick a woman whose hysteria will suppress your own need to express.

However, it's one thing to pick the right person—it's another to keep love alive. In regard to finally coming home to love, there are two important things to remember: Love isn't perfect and love takes work.

Real love, love that can last a lifetime, isn't perfect. Even the man or woman of your dreams will have flaws. Real love does not ignore the imperfections; it acknowledges them but doesn't become obsessed by them because the joys of the relationship so far outweigh the flaws. The relationship you've just ended is over not because it wasn't perfect, but because after your developmental tasks were complete, there were significant, unbridgeable differences. It wasn't 5 or 25 percent inappropriate; it was 50 or 60 or 80 percent inappropriate. A viable relationship, on the other hand, feels generally appropriate and is focused on what the couple has in common, not their differences.

Love that lasts takes work. Our ended relationships often point up what poor stewards we have been of our loves. So often we're lazy about love and take our relationships for granted. It's almost as if having set them up, we assume they'll run automatically—we take better care of our lawnmowers and cars!

Relationships are living things—they require tending. Like plants, they flourish when they are cared for. Our ended relationships remind us of how much nurturing was withheld, how many resentments piled up, how much communication never occurred, how many needs went unfulfilled. They challenge us to see how we were lazy last time and what we must do differently in order to cultivate our next relationship.

What I'm saying is that love—the butterflies in the stomach emotion—does not conquer all. Real love, enduring love, love that forms and informs a lasting relationship, is more than a fast-food fix of good feeling. It is the quiet recognition and ongoing appreciation of another person, the experience of continually sharing what is important to you. When we love, we love the other who most fully gives us an experience of our best and most essential self.

You will love and have a happy life with the person whose looks, nature, habits, preferences, values, and priorities call forth the truest expression of yourself, the person who invites you to blossom and grow. It is with this person that you truly have the potential of enjoying a relationship "till death do you part."

11

A Ritual for Parting

THIS IS A RITUAL TO BE PERFORMED with the person with whom you are ending or have already ended a relationship. If that person isn't available or doesn't want to do it, you should do the exercises in chapter 9, because this ceremony is designed for a shared completion.

The ceremony here can be done sometime during the process of parting, as a ritual to mark the completion, or it can be done much later, after the dust has settled, as a way of initiating another form of relationship between the two of you. In either case, you will want to create specific guidelines on how to move forward with your new, separated relationship. For example, two people may do the ritual, then agree not to see or talk to each other for a month, and then explore the possibility of reconnecting in some new way. Or they may say, now that we've done the ritual, let's go out to dinner as friends and begin our friendship right now. Or you may agree that after you do this ceremony, you will not see each other ever again. What's important is that you come to a mutual decision.

This ritual can also be used as the final step of healing by people who ended their relationship long ago. I know one couple who used it to resolve a relationship that ended twenty years before. Neither had been able to find a true love, but several months after completing the ceremony, they each met the person whom later they would marry.

Whether you use it as an instrument of completion or to resolve lingering feelings from a relationship that ended years ago makes no difference. You will intuitively know when the time is right. Either way, it will bring you a feeling of deep resolution and the opportunity to begin again.

Decide on a time and a place together. You may want to do it in one of your houses or apartments—a place where you lived out your relationship—or you may prefer to conduct in it a place that is new to both of you—a park, the quiet back room of a restaurant, or even a church sanctuary. It should be a place that will not unnecessarily arouse negative feelings. Pick a day when you will have enough time. It's also nice when you're doing this to have candles and music or some other influences that confer peace and neutrality, such as incense or flowers. Many people choose to bring a gift to one another, a small token that will symbolize this completion in the future, as well as remind you, in a tender, thoughtful way, of the pleasures and the depth you shared.

Above all, take time. Don't rush through the questions. Allow each person to speak his or her piece for as long as it takes. Many people have finally learned, through the openings provided by this ritual, some of the missing information or feelings about their relationship—revelations that allowed them to receive its gifts and let it go more easily.

You will also want to make a specific plan in advance for what you are going to do after the completion of the ceremony. For example, to go to a movie together, walk out of the church where you've quietly had this conversation, or leave your former sweetheart's home for the last time. It's best to arrange this beforehand so that the impact of the ceremony isn't diluted at the end by returning to a trivial discussion of "what should we do now?"

The usual format is for one person to ask the other a question and then listen to the response. Then the respondent asks the other person the same question. This way both people have an opportunity to discover and savor what is the same and different in their experience. After the respondent makes a revelation, you may say, "Thank you for telling me that," or, "I never knew. It's good (or surprising or wonderful) to know how that was for you." A short response is appropriate, but not a long response or a rebuttal. You are not here to hash over old ground again, but truly to hear what the other person has to say.

Remember to do this with love. Your relationship is over. Nothing's going to change that. This is your opportunity to step into a higher level of love and appreciation. May you find the real meaning of your time together and may you release one another with thanksgiving and joy.

The Questions

1. Just for the joy of it, tell me at what point in our relationship you "fell in love" with me.

2. For you, what was the sweetest time we ever had together? (Event, shared experience, touching moment.)

3. What was the incident or experience that broke your trust and caused you to start withdrawing from our relationship?
Did we ever solve that or is it still a painful issue for you?

   (The person who is asking the question should now say, "I'm so sorry. Please forgive me." Or, "I hope someday you will feel resolved about it.")

4. What did you like best about our life together? (For example, "Our home life." "Raising the kids together." "Dancing." "Our sexual relationship." "The trips we took."
   (Thank him for that; thank her for that.)

5. For you, what was the healing in our relationship? What are the things you learned? What were the most important things I gave you? How have you changed because of our love?
   For example, you might say, "For me the healing was the nurturing and mothering you gave me. I needed this so much and I didn't even know it until you gave it to me with such endless generosity. Thank you for allowing me to be a child, so I could finally grow up. Thank you for mothering me, even when you got tired of it. Your nurturing saved my life. I feel strong enough now to take the next step because of it."

6. What is the hurt you have never been able to mention to me?
   For example, "That you didn't come with me to have the abortion. I was so shocked I was never able to mention it." Or, "That you were never able to accept my parents."
   After they have revealed it, apologize. For example, "I'm so sorry. I never realized how much that hurt you. Thank you for finally telling me."

7. What has been the greatest relief about ending this relationship?
   For example, you might say, "That I don't have to wonder anymore whether or not you'll ever decide to marry me. Now I can just appreciate you from a distance."

8. What are you afraid of never having again with anyone else?
   "The depth." "The great sex." "Sharing the kids in a day to day way."

9. Finally, tell each other that you release one another to a new relationship—a new relationship with someone else and a different relationship with each other. Say what you would like your new relationship to be.

   For example, "I'd like us to be friends now." Or, "I'd like us to spend a month apart and then get together for dinner and talk about what's happened to each of us." Or even, "I'm glad we had this ceremony, but losing you is so painful for me that I really need to not see you again. If that changes sometime, I'll let you know, but for me, I really need this to be an ending without any plans for the future."

10. Then, in your own words, find a way to express that because you have loved each other (and because in some sense you still do), and in gratitude for what you have learned and become with one another, it's now all right to seek love with someone else. Remind each other that the new love will never erase the love that the two of you have shared, or separate you from one another at the deepest level. It's time now, though, to pass on the gifts you received from each other. It's time to move on.

    For example, "You nurtured me so wonderfully that now I feel able to love a child," or, "Your appreciation of me as a woman has given me the confidence I need to try to take singing lessons," or, "Your support of my career has made me willing to risk applying for that new job."

11. Finally, embrace or kiss each other, and say, "Thank you for loving me as long and as well as you did." If it feels appropriate, you can even say, "I'll always love you."

When your ceremony is complete, say good-bye and follow the plans you set up before you began it, that is, to go out to dinner, to say good-bye at the door, to walk out of the church facing different directions, or to say good night and both walk out to your cars in the parking lot with no plans to see one another again.

Allow some personal time to absorb the feelings that this ceremony has generated. If your plan is *not* to be together, you may want to go to a quiet place, and in a notebook or journal, write down the feelings that the ceremony generated for you and your hopes for the future.

May this ritual of loving departure be the portal to new love for you.

A Diagnostic Coda

When Love No Longer Works—Signs and Symptoms of Ending

THIS CODA IS FOR YOU if you are in a relationship that is floundering or making you unhappy enough to wonder whether or not it is ending or should end. In their heart of hearts, people always know when their relationships are ending. At some level, we all know everything that is going on in our lives, but often we prefer not to tell ourselves what we know. One of the reasons we hide from the truth is that it is terribly painful to end a relationship. We would much prefer to keep our heads in the sand, to try as much as possible to ignore the problems, which may be the indications of terminal trouble, so we can avoid the pain we are sure lies ahead.

As a result, we allow a lot of unpleasant, painful, and even unbearable things to go on in our relationships; we don't know if they are things we should endure or are symptomatic of a relationship that really should end.

Relationships should enhance our lives, and although even at best they include unpleasant experiences, when the majority of the experiences are unpleasant, then questions about the viability of the relationship need to be raised. This coda is designed to help you identify whether or not the things you are observing and feeling are indicators that, in fact, your relationships is ending or is only going through some growing pains. If your relationship has already ended, this coda may help you clarify the reasons why it did.

Fights

One of the indicators of a relationship in trouble is that it has become a battleground. "All we do is fight; we can't have a single normal conversation." When this is an accurate description of your relationship, the only experience you're really sharing is conflict. There may still be short interludes in which you share a social event, a sexual encounter, or a recreational experience with your children, but basically the majority of your intimate contact is in the battle zone. Instead of sharing good feelings, every encounter is an opportunity to express your rage and disappointment—how your partner failed you in the past and continues to fail you in the present.

When a relationship gets to this point, it usually means that its life-giving, nourishing elements have been depleted, and it has moved into the degenerative phase.

It may be that along with the fighting there are one or two other strands of connection that still bind you together. For example, one woman said, "We fight all the time, but our sex life is still fantastic." Such a remark can indicate a number of things. At the simplest level, it indicates that conflict often enhances the sexual experience. It also shows that we are so afraid of ending our relationships that we cling to anything that supports our hope that they can be revitalized.

While fighting can be a positive thing within a flourishing relationship, repetitive, purposeless fighting more often indicates that a relationship is ending.

In a healthy relationship, although there may be several repetitions of a given conflict, eventually some insight occurs or some new information is revealed so that the partners know more about each other, feel closer to each other, and will conduct their relationship differently in the future because of the insight that has occurred. When fighting is indicative of the end of a relationship, however, it is essentially nonproductive. Nothing is illuminated, and the combatants come away from the conflict feeling as if they have watched, for the two-thousandth time, the very same frame of a movie they have seen for years. Instead of feeling closer after the fight, they finish it feeling estranged from each other and totally hopeless about their situation.

One of the reasons people endure the two-thousandth rerun of their conflict is that it is reasonable to hope that repetition will produce results. However, if there is no change whatsoever in each succeeding version of the fight, if the same emotional territory is being gone over time and time again, you are probably fighting just to avoid the end of your relationship.

Irreconcilable Differences

In a number of states the term "irreconcilable differences" has become the grounds for divorce, and certainly irreconcilable differences are indicators that a relationship is moving toward its conclusion.

A couple is experiencing irreconcilable differences when either one of them finds that the area of common ground they once shared is now so small that what occupies that territory is a multitude of differences.

You may find, for instance, that your activities are different, your habits are different, your friends are different, your values are different, your preferred vacations are different, and basically the only thing you still have in common is that you are the person who can identify how different the other person is from you.

Irreconcilable differences occur in certain strategic areas. A common one is time—how much time each partner wants to commit to the intimate life of the relationship. Some people want a relationship that consists of a weekend date or two weekday dates and nothing else, while for another person the very definition of a relationship is daily intimate conversations, with a lot of time spent together, and many loving exchanges.

This points to another area of potential conflict, namely, the amount of commitment each person is willing to make to the relationship. Because people are trying to meet their individual needs through a relationship, there is often a significant discrepancy in the kind and amount of commitment each partner is willing to make. In general, the conflict tends to divide along gender lines, with women being willing to commit themselves unequivocally in terms of time, service, and compromise, and men less willing to do so.

The conflict about commitment generally finds women complaining that their men are never home, that they never do thoughtful or romantic things, and that they aren't willing to give up their golf games, their business meetings, or their nights out with the boys, whereas women are willing to drop everything for love. Men, on the other hand, complain that women are clingy and dependent, that they are never content merely to be loved, and that they have no distinct identity outside of their relationships.

A corollary issue of commitment has to do with whether or not people are going to live together. Again, dividing along gender lines, women tend to want to live together more often than the men they love. Many relationships founder because the man was never willing to go from dating to living together or from living together to marriage.

While each partner can and must compromise to a certain degree, when the joint compromise fails to land the relationship in a comfortable middle ground, it is likely that the relationship will not survive. There is a limit to the amount of compromise we can make and still preserve our integrity—and sanity.

Other irreconcilable differences have to do with cultural tastes, personal values, or geographic differences. For example, you may discover that he really wants to live the life of a homesteader in the country while you love the urban life with its neon-electric pace, or you realize that you have embraced a religion that she could never accept. If you really must move to New York City to become a photographer and she can't bear the thought, you have what is essentially an irresolvable conflict.

Often conflicts have to do with money. When his wife received her sizable inheritance, one man felt suddenly totally inadequate. "There was no way I could possibly feel important to her anymore. My work and my capacity to provide no longer had any meaning at all. I felt like a worthless person."

Radical physical changes may also create an unbridgeable rift. "When John fell off the roof, broke his back, and became a paraplegic, as terrible as it sounds, I simply couldn't handle it. I kept remembering him as he used to be, and I couldn't make the adjustment."

Even though we use the term "irreconcilable differences" cavalierly to describe why relationships end, it is nevertheless true that sometimes people arrive at a place where their differences cannot be bridged by compromise, negotiation, or goodwill. At this point, the differences are truly irreconcilable, and as often as not they indicate that a relationship has completed its cycle.

Boredom

One of the ways you can tell it's ending is that one day you may get up feeling depressed, vaguely disconnected, and blue. "I don't know why," you may say to yourself, "but it feels like life isn't worth living. I'm bored and depressed. I don't know what's the matter with me. Nothing terrible has happened, but I just have this creepy, listless, hopeless feeling."

When you feel this way, it could be that the essential vitality in your relationship is gone. The thrill is gone; the zing has zung; there's nothing happening between you two. You're not "in love" anymore, and you're also not having enough ongoing transactions that have meaning or provide sufficient nourishment for your relationship to be alive and well.

It may be that you've drawn away from each other gradually, by such imperceptible increments, that without your even noticing the change, you have both gone off into separate worlds. Or maybe something dramatic has happened to push you apart. No matter what the vehicle of your removal from one another, essentially your relationship is no longer a resource anymore.

The feelings that go along with this kind of slow demise of a relationship are a lack of focus and a lack of purpose. But how do you know, you might ask, that your relationship is the reason why you're so bored? There's a lot of boredom in life, and even people who are happily in love sometimes wake up bored, listless, and feeling as if life hasn't got a purpose and nothing wonderful, exciting, or captivating is ever going to happen again.

It is true that boredom and restlessness in and of themselves are not necessarily indicative of problems in a relationship, nor do they necessarily indicate that it is moving toward its conclusion. Life is sometimes boring, and even when we are in love, it is often frustrating. In general, however, when you are feeling bored and frustrated about your life—and not your relationship—your partner will serve as a refuge from all those awful feelings; your relationship will be a healing and comforting place. Your sweetheart will be the person to whom you turn to talk about your frustrating job, the children's problems at school, or the endless stream of mechanical failures you've recently been plagued with.

When it's the relationship itself that isn't working, however, you find yourself turning away from your partner. You find that all your significant nourishment is coming from other sources. "Suddenly everything about him bored me," one of my clients said. "I couldn't remember or feel a single thing about him that excited me or captured my attention."

Divining whether it's your relationship or life itself that is causing your boredom takes a certain amount of research. You have to locate the source of your boredom by asking yourself: "Am I bored when I go to work? No, I feel pretty good when I get behind my desk. It's when I come home that I start feeling bad. I don't come home with joy, expectation, or anticipation. I open a beer and read the paper. I have my dinner and watch TV. I sit around and read magazines, but none of it has any pulling power for me. I'm avoiding the person I supposedly love. I'm not seeing him or her as a plus in my life anymore."

Since it's easy for us to make relationships take the blame for everything, to assume that the person closest to us is the cause of everything that's wrong or disappointing in life, it's very important to check out all the other external factors. Are the feelings you're experiencing the result of some difficult or changing circumstance in your non-intimate outside world, or are these feelings really a result of having come to the finishing place in your relationship? If nothing else registers on your emotional Richter scale, maybe it is that your relationship is ending.

Sometimes the end of a relationship creeps up slowly like a change in the weather, a storm gathering in the distance. "I got to the point where I woke up every morning saying to myself, 'Oh, my God, another day.'" said one of my woman clients. "It wasn't that anything terrible was happening. It was that nothing was happening.

"We weren't fighting. We didn't have money problems; our sex was functional, though not particularly exciting. Our house was pleasant enough and paid for. Our children were doing well enough in school—and yet I found myself with the old is-that-all-there-is feeling most of the time.

"It was the sense that life would go on like this, unchanging, forever, that really depressed me, and I realized that I was in a marriage where there wasn't any spark, and there hadn't been any for a long, long time.

"Even after seeing that, I wondered if it really was my marriage," this woman went on, "so I looked at everything and everyone else in my life until I was satisfied that Phil and I didn't have anything in common anymore. When I saw that we really didn't, I knew it wasn't appropriate for us to be together any longer. I knew then that the end was in sight. From that point on I realized that there would be no going back. I didn't know how we would end or what would precipitate it, but I knew our relationship was over."

As my client's story indicates, it's terribly important to stop and identify whether what you are feeling is truly boredom or simply familiarity. When we first fall in love, there is always a feeling of excitement. The relationship is thrilling; there is incredible sexual energy; there are great expectations. As time goes on, however, these feelings mellow, and then it's important to discover whether the ensuing excitement means the relationship has settled into its comfortable long-term rhythm or whether real boredom has set in.

There is an important difference between boredom and familiarity. It's like the difference between an old shoe that's comfortable and a shoe that's worn out and has started to hurt your feet. When a relationship has settled but still has liveliness, you don't experience true boredom; what you experience is familiarity, comfort, security. You value your daily involvement with the other person. You view your partner as a resource and an ally and think to yourself, "I know I can talk to him about it," or "I know she'll understand." When you no longer see your partner as a resource or an ally, or when your partner is no longer interesting to you, then you are genuinely bored.

Emotional Distance

For most people, boredom is the most pervasive feeling that indicates a relationship is on its way out. But sometimes the feeling is much more acute. You become aware that the person to whom you've been relating is no longer there when you reach out to make contact. You try to have a conversation but you get no response, or you try to have a conversation and get a consistently negative response. You have sex that is no longer binding in any wonderful way, you have sex that doesn't even arouse a negative feeling in you because there's so much distance that you can no longer even be hurt, or you feel that you're trying to make contact, but the other person isn't there.

This is what people mean when they refer to "a lack of communication." Verbal communication—what we say to one another and how we say it, the amount and depth of our revelations about ourselves, the spirit in which we say what we say—is one of the most important means of sustaining emotional closeness. When there is a breakdown in any form of communication—verbal, sexual, affectional, emotional—there is a breakdown in the relationship that is experienced as emotional distance.

Emotional distance occurs when you come to the place in your own consciousness where, for whatever reasons, you have moved away from your relationship. You are, in a sense, holding back your emotions and expending them elsewhere. It's as if you've got money, but you're not spending it at your partner's store anymore; you're shopping somewhere else. You're having your essential interactions somewhere else: in your work, in your private time with yourself, in your church, in your bowling league, with one or many special friends. For whatever reasons, you've decided to limit the depth of your contact with your partner.

"One day I realized that I hadn't said anything important to him for years," June said. "Without even knowing it, I had stopped telling him everything important. One day I realized I had changed so much that he really didn't know me anymore. I'd become a totally different person—a total stranger to him."

When we investigated what had happened, June discovered that several years ago she had said something important to her husband. She'd told him she wanted to go back to school and get a master's degree in business management, and he'd said, "That's just another one of your harebrained schemes. You don't have time for that."

That particular remark was a turning point for her, the moment at which she started withdrawing from her husband. She didn't enroll in the master's program, but she did start taking the classes that would prepare her for it—and she took them without telling him. It was his disinterest in her whereabouts that marked the second phase of her emotional withdrawal. "Where were you?" he'd sometimes ask, and when she answered, "At a class," and he didn't inquire about it, she removed herself even further. "I realized that he really wasn't interested in what I was trying to make of myself. From that point on my classes became my secret life. I stopped sharing everything, except the most boring, trivial matters with him. I don't know why it affected me so terribly, his calling my idea about graduate school a harebrained scheme, but it did."

Tony, a middle-aged businessman, had a similar experience. "It was when I realized she wasn't willing to struggle with me that I withdrew from her," he said. "She wanted all the rewards. She wanted me to be rich, she wanted the big house and the big cars, the Cartier watch, and the trips to Europe; but back there at the beginning, she wasn't willing to be at the bottom with me.

"I had a fantastic business idea—and support for it from a whole lot of total strangers—but she just pooh-poohed it. So I took my scheme and went underground. I completely stopped talking to her about it but I didn't give up. I decided it was mine, it wasn't part of our marriage anymore.

"You know," he concluded, "when we were finally getting a divorce a year later—and by then I had lined up a whole set of investors and was ready to go into production with my item—she said to me, 'Oh, by the way, whatever happened to that idea of yours, did you ever do anything with it?' We were so detached during the last year and a half of our marriage that she didn't have the vaguest idea of what I was doing."

Sometimes the process of emotional withdrawal isn't even a process. It's the carrying forward of a status quo, the continuance of an emotional bonding that never occurred. Nan and Rob came for counseling, which ended up being more like the last rites for a twelve-year marriage in which they had communicated virtually nothing to one another. In fact, I began to feel as if I were the person who actually got them acquainted with each other. They had lived twelve years of all form and no content, and it was only because a proposed job transfer for Rob got them talking that they finally came for counseling and realized how incompatible they had always been. As we explored their relationship, they were amazed that they had married one another, much less that they had managed to live in the same house for a dozen years. Emotional distance had been the hallmark, the very essence of their relationship, and when reality intervened, requiring them to reveal their true feelings, they were unable to find enough common ground.

Rob was organized, an intellectual, and a perfectionist. He liked life to be under control. Nan was a clown; she liked a free-form, spontaneous life, changing her mind in an instant, pursuing whatever captured her fancy.

When the day of reckoning came, they found that, in fact, they disliked each other's values and the choices their respective values represented. "You mean, you really think the kids don't need to learn how to make their own beds?" Rob raved. "You mean you really think we should be saving a third of our income?" Nan gasped. In therapy, they identified these and many other differences as irreconcilable and eventually agreed upon a divorce that was as emotionally detached as their marriage had been.

Deep emotional distance is often an indicator that there is no turning back in a relationship, that on an unconscious level both partners have already created an alternate private reality based on their differing values. Once this has happened, they also stop consulting each other about creating a joint reality that serves both their needs.

The recognition of an emotional separation is often a very painful one, and it is frequently accompanied by feelings of shock that are similar to those people feel when they are notified of a death. "Suddenly, he wasn't there anymore." "Suddenly, she was gone." There's a feeling of loss. It's as if someone with whom you had dreamed your whole future has, without your quite knowing it, been taken away.

Changes in Venue

Many relationships that have already outlived their usefulness really flounder and collapse when there is a change in the geographical circumstance of the relationship. Since we generally carry on our relationships in a daily and domestic fashion, there is much about a relationship that is supported by and contained within its specific geographical and domestic circumstances.

When a relationship has already passed its vital state, a change in location or circumstance can bring out the fact that all the essential underpinnings in the relationship are already gone, that in a sense the relationship was being held together by the house, the neighborhood, or the town. Very often people will say, "We built our dream house and then we got divorced," or "It was after we left the apartment on 43rd Street that everything started falling apart," or "When we moved to Ohio, nothing seemed right anymore."

People always say these things with a vague sense of surprise, an unfocused awareness—like, oh, it seems like something happened there, but of course, it didn't really happen. Or did it? Oh my God, maybe it did. Although they are reporting it to me as if they had known it all along, it's clear that they themselves have never before taken note of the fact that changing houses or moving from one town to another has had incredible impact on their relationship, has changed it utterly, in fact.

My point here is that changes in circumstance, while not in themselves harbingers of doom for any relationship, are very often stocktaking times. Major changes of this kind often precipitate crises that cannot be solved or become special transitional times in which longstanding, irresolvable differences are finally identified.

For Bob and Jane, for example, this critical time occurred when they moved to California. Bob had finished graduate school in the East, and both he and Jane agreed that it was time for a new beginning. With high hopes they set out across the country. They bought and lavishly decorated what they both believed would be their dream house, but it turned into a house of horror as years of conflict, suppressed while Bob was in school, began to surface.

Bob had always been dissatisfied with their sex life and initiated an affair with a younger woman. Jane had always disliked the way he'd behaved as a father and started vigorously complaining. Now that graduate school was over and it was time, in her opinion, to launch into family life, she found him unacceptable. Within six months of their arrival, they were deep in the marital crisis that resulted in divorce a year later.

For Pam and Bill it was different. A return to the town of her childhood reminded her of who she'd been before she was married. As she put it, "Somehow when I returned to the familiar environment, I remembered that once I'd been somebody other than Mrs. So-and-So. I got back in touch with myself and realized that for years I hadn't been myself with Bill. Suddenly my marriage seemed irrelevant."

The stress of change has the effect of bringing to light all the things that were not, in fact, alive and well in a relationship. Facing these challenges becomes an occasion for growth, for improving the relationship and making the transition to its next chapter if the relationship is still viable and only needs some dusting off. Or perhaps facing these challenges becomes the occasion for acknowledging that the relationship is ending or has ended long ago.

I mention this specifically because when people have uncomfortable feelings about moving across the country or moving to a different house or changing neighborhoods, it often really is an indicator that the relationship is ending. This possibility, while surprising to each person who mentions it, is so common an indicator of the ending of a relationship that it always needs to be taken seriously.

Affairs

Affairs, of course, are the classic indicators that something isn't right with a relationship. Sex is a very binding component of any relationship, and for most of us, it is still what separates a permanent love relationship from a friendship or a romantic dalliance. In general, we have agreed that sexual bonding is one of the ways we define our primary relationships. For this reason, it generally does have a divisive and corrosive effect when we dilute our commitment by having sex outside of our primary relationship. When we do that, we take away one of the things that makes that particular relationship unique and exclusive. This can't help but affect the primary relationship. We all know this on an unconscious level. That's one of the reasons why, when we are trying to end a relationship but don't know how, we often engage in an affair. Unconsciously we know that the affair will communicate our real intentions—intentions which are still unfocused or which we're afraid to express in a more direct way.

"Looking back, I really don't know why I got involved with Cindy," Dave said. "She isn't my type. She turned out to be a pinhead intellectually, and yet I found myself sort of irrevocably drawn to her. When Sue found out, I couldn't defend myself. It became weirdly clear that I had needed a way out of my relationship with her, so I got involved with this girl half my age, someone I really had no interest in, just so Sue would find out and I would finally be able to tell her that I wanted out of the marriage. Totally backwards, huh? But I guess I didn't know how else to do it. I didn't do it intentionally, mind you. But looking back, I can see that's what I was really doing."

"This wasn't even my first affair," said Lee Ann of the long-term affair that finally ended her marriage. "I'd had another affair, a real heartbreaker, seven years ago. Larry and I were in trouble even then. We had some marriage counseling that didn't seem to get anywhere, but frankly, I was too scared to break up the marriage. The kids were still little and I was afraid to strike out on my own, so I just went off and had my wonderful affair. When my lover moved out of town, I was devastated. I was suddenly grateful that I still had my marriage, bad as it was, and I swore I'd never get involved with anyone else again.

"Then Ed came along, and before I could remember my resolution, we were heavily involved. It was primarily sexual—I never thought of having a future with him. Then, one day I thought to myself: 'I'm going to get caught, and I'm going to lose them both.'

"And that's exactly what happened. I was amazed by my own predictions. Now, of course, I realize that I wanted to get caught. It was almost a relief when Larry found out.

"I used Ed to help me make the new beginning. The minute Larry found out about my affair, I was instantly no longer interested in Ed. Suddenly, the real reason I was involved with him was embarrassingly clear—he was a tool, a vehicle for me to end my marriage."

Multiple or repeated affairs usually indicate a basic incompatibility. "I've had a million affairs," Tom said, obviously exaggerating. "I've had more sex with strangers than I've ever had with my wife. Our marriage was doomed from the start. It was sort of a set-up marriage, then the kids came along, and then it was curtains. No way out. I was trapped.

"I did try at the beginning to be faithful. But it didn't work. We were incompatible every which way. She was really ambitious; I'm just an easy-going guy. I don't even know why we got married. It was the time, I guess. We were both just out of high school. She was the prettiest girl around. And besides, there wasn't anything else to do. Even our parents liked the idea; they liked the idea of marriage keeping us off the streets.

"What finally happened was that I had an affair with a really sweet young girl. She fell in love with me, and I broke her heart, and that really got to me. I came to my senses. I said to myself, 'You're not having a marriage, you're just going around using people because you are too chicken to face your life.' That night I went home and confessed. I told my wife I wanted a divorce, and you know what, that was the first real conversation she and I ever had."

The marriage that is constantly punctuated by affairs is not a marriage or an intimate relationship, it is a circumstantial arrangement and will survive only as long as both partners are content to have a marriage of convenience. When either partner desires to change the arrangement into a truly intimate emotional relationship, chances are it won't work because the emotional territory has already been violated by so many imposters.

Sometimes the affair stands for incomplete or impossible communication that can't be created between the partners, and sometimes the affair stands for communication that hasn't been allowed within the person who's having the affair. What I mean by this is that sometimes people don't even know their marriage is in trouble until they find themselves having an affair. The affair serves to teach the person his or her emotional truth: "Oh, I must not really want to be married anymore." Very often, the person of whom this is true, if asked the day before he commenced his affair if he was happy in his marriage, would have said, "Of course. I'm as happy as anyone else."

In general, the incorporation of outside sexual relationships into a marriage or primary relationship is a sign that the primary relationship is in trouble—or as one of my clients once said: "Open marriage is practice divorce."

If you are the person whose partner is having the affair, however, it's not quite so easy to be philosophical about it, to see it simply as a garbled attempt at communication. Because affairs touch us at some of our deepest and most vulnerable emotional levels, we tend to treat them as ultimate reflections on the character of the persons who engage in them.

People who indulge in affairs may indeed be selfish, self-indulgent, and inconsiderate. But what is also and more importantly true is that affairs may not be so much a statement about individual character as they are about the quality of the relationships upon which they inevitably impinge.

Counseling or Therapy

Marital and relationship crises often provide the occasion in which people finally seek therapy. Unfortunately, however, by the time the ragged couple arrives, it is usually not time to create or restore a relationship, but rather to bid it a conscious and conscientious farewell.

It doesn't please me to list marriage counseling as one of the indicators of a relationship that is ending, but I think it is important to note that generally people seek therapy only when they have already crossed their own interior limits of problem-solving capabilities. That's why counseling—a process which ideally would heal and restore a relationship—is just as often a process by which a couple brings a relationship to its conclusion. Thus, because many people seek counseling when it's already too late, what they need is help in extricating themselves from an unworkable situation. I think that's a good reason to come for counseling—more people should—because there's a real conscience operating there that says, "I've loved this person, I've spent an important part of my life with him or her, and I want to find a way to end this epoch gracefully and graciously."

I certainly don't mean to say that people only come for counseling when their marriages are ending, because there are people with foresight who seek therapy as a resource for relationships that are working fairly well but need a little tidying up. But let me repeat: People very often come for counseling only because their relationship is over and they don't know how to tell one another, or they haven't been able to face it themselves.

Relationships do end—even though we don't want to believe it. Whether you have obscured that truth from yourself by having an affair or enduring years of boredom, whether you have been starved for emotional communion or have never been able to recover from a move—if you think your relationship is ending, you're probably right.

Because the ending of a relationship is so painful, so unthinkable, we don't acknowledge the possibility to ourselves, even speculatively, unless it's probably true. We don't play around with our perceptions at this devastating level unless they are based on reality. When we've entertained these cataclysmic perceptions and felt the terror associated with them, it is only then, in therapy or by ourselves, that we can begin the painful process of ending the relationship and resolving our feelings about it.

If after reading this coda, you feel that your relationship is ending, begin with chapter 1 to unravel the meanings of your relationship and to learn how to live through its ending.

About the Author

Adam Latham

Daphne Rose Kingma, an undisputed expert on matters of the heart, is a best-selling author, counselor, life coach, and spiritual guide. Her books include: *Finding True Love, The Men We Never Knew, True Love, The Future of Love* and *The Ten Things To Do When Your Life Falls Apart: An Emotional and Spiritual Handbook*. Her books have sold over one million copies and been translated into fifteen languages.

Dubbed "The Love Doctor" by the *San Francisco Chronicle*, Daphne has been a six-time guest on Oprah as well as numerous other television shows and hundreds of radio programs. Her work has appeared in a host of newspapers and magazines including *Mademoiselle, Self, Cosmopolitan,* the *Los Angeles Times*, and *The Dallas Morning News*.

A charismatic speaker and workshop leader, she inspires audiences throughout the U.S. and Europe and regularly conducts workshops at the Esalen Institute, Big Sur, California and at Hollyhock, Cortes Island, British Columbia. She lives in Santa Barbara, California.

To learn more, inquire about keynotes, personal sessions, books, and audio books, or to join Daphne's mailing list, visit: *www.daphnekingma.com.*

Follow Daphne on Twitter: *www.twitter.com/#!/daphne_kingma* and Facebook: *www.facebook.com/daphne.kingma*

To Our Readers

Conari Press, an imprint of Red Wheel/Weiser, publishes books on topics ranging from spirituality, personal growth, and relationships to women's issues, parenting, and social issues. Our mission is to publish quality books that will make a difference in people's lives—how we feel about ourselves and how we relate to one another. We value integrity, compassion, and receptivity, both in the books we publish and in the way we do business.

Our readers are our most important resource, and we appreciate your input, suggestions, and ideas about what you would like to see published.

Visit our website, *www.redwheelweiser.com*, where you can learn about our upcoming books and free downloads, and be sure to go to *www.redwheelweiser.com/newsletter/* to sign up for newsletters and exclusive offers.

You can also contact us at *info@redwheelweiser.com*.

Conari Press
an imprint of Red Wheel/Weiser, LLC
665 Third Street, Suite 400
San Francisco, CA 94107